NEW JERSEY

DMV EXAM

WORKBOOK

400+ PRACTICE QUESTIONS TO NAVIGATE YOUR DMV EXAM WITH CONFIDENCE

CONTENT

INTRODUCTION

Welcome and thank you for choosing our workbook as your trusted companion on your journey to achieving your driver's license. This meticulously designed resource is not just a book, but a complete guide intended to empower you with the knowledge, confidence, and practice necessary to ace the DMV test.

This workbook is crafted with a careful selection of questions derived directly from the Driver's Manual of your respective state. Each question has been thoughtfully constructed to cover key areas of the exam, providing a comprehensive understanding of every aspect you'll be tested on. Our primary aim is to help you fully grasp the material, turning any uncertainties into strengths.

Here are some strategic steps to ensure you make the most of this valuable resource:

1. **Consistent Practice:** Begin by taking the practice tests in one sitting, from start to finish, replicating the actual exam conditions. This will not only test your knowledge but also build your endurance and help you manage time effectively.
2. **Detailed Review:** Post completion, focus on the questions you answered incorrectly. The answer key, located at the back of this book, provides clear explanations for each question. Understanding your mistakes is a critical part of the learning process and will significantly improve your performance.
3. **Regular Revision:** As the saying goes, "Repetition is the mother of learning." Regular revision will reinforce your knowledge and help you remember information for longer periods.
4. **Mock Exams:** Once you've thoroughly studied and revised the material, take the practice tests again. This time, aim for higher scores. Gradually, you will see your understanding deepen and your scores improve.
5. **Stay Updated:** Laws and regulations can change. It's crucial to ensure you're studying the most recent information. Check online resources or contact your local DMV for updates.

Remember, the journey to success lies in persistent and intelligent practice. The more you engage with the material, the better you will understand it, and the more comfortable you'll be during the actual DMV exam.

For every question in this workbook, you'll find a corresponding answer accompanied by a detailed explanation. In instances where multiple answers may seem correct, we've included a comprehensive explanation for each response. This approach will help you understand not only why the correct answer is indeed correct, but also why the other options are incorrect. This level of understanding is what separates those who merely pass from those who excel.

We believe that with dedication, practice, and the right guidance, anyone can master the skills required to pass the DMV test. This workbook is your map to that journey. Good luck on your path to becoming a confident and responsible driver!

THE NEW JERSEY DRIVER'S HANDBOOK

The NEW JERSEY Department of Motor Vehicles strongly recommends that all test takers familiarize themselves with the official manual. This comprehensive guide offers an in-depth understanding of the rules, regulations, and knowledge required to pass your exam. It is suggested that you read through this manual at least once to familiarize yourself with the necessary content.

To access this invaluable resource, simply scan the provided QR code or type the link into your browser to download it.

https://www.state.nj.us/mvc/about/manuals.htm

CHEAT SHEETS
In addition to the official handbook, we have included Cheat Sheets in this workbook. These are specifically designed to assist you in reviewing the top 100 questions commonly seen on the DMV written test. These Cheat Sheets serve as a quick reference guide and a powerful review tool, making them an indispensable resource in the days leading up to your exam. You will find them conveniently located at the end of the book, right before the Answer Sheets.

We wholeheartedly wish you the best of luck on your journey towards obtaining your driver's license. To maximize your chances of success, we encourage you to take our practice tests as many times as necessary. Remember, consistent practice is the key to mastery!

There's no time like the present. Start studying today and embark on your path to acing your DMV exam! We thank you once again for choosing this book as your trusted guide, and we hope it assists you in reaching your driving objectives.

As a final note, we would love to hear about your learning journey. Please consider writing a review of the book. Your feedback is invaluable in helping us refine our resources and better assist future drivers on their path to success.

BONUSES

THE TOP 100 MOST FAQs

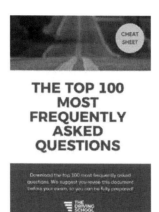

Get access to our compilation of the 100 most commonly asked questions on the DMV exam. We strongly recommend you review this valuable resource prior to your test day, ensuring your readiness for the most likely questions to come your way! Keep in mind, the more you rehearse, the more refined your performance will be on the actual DMV test.

To retrieve this resource, simply enter the provided link into your browser or make use of the QR Code for swift access.

- https://dl.bookfunnel.com/lhf68zpx12

200 BONUS PRACTICE QUESTIONS

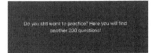

"Master the DMV: Bonus Practice Questions" is a comprehensive collection of additional, carefully crafted questions that mirror the variety, style, and complexity of the ones you'll encounter in the real DMV exam. Perhaps you've already completed the questions in our main guide and are yearning for more practice. Or maybe you just want to challenge yourself and ensure no stone is left unturned in your preparations. Regardless of your motivation, this bonus eBook is your perfect ally.

To retrieve this resource, simply enter the provided link into your browser or make use of the QR Code for swift access.

https://dl.bookfunnel.com/l15oxwpd9e

PRACTICE TEST 1

Gear up for the DMV driving permit test by engaging with practice questions that bear a striking resemblance (and are frequently identical!) to the ones you'll encounter on the actual DMV exam.

Total Questions: 40
Correct Answer to pass: 32

Question 1 - Practice Test 1

To legally drive a moped, you must be at least 15 years old and possess _____.

- ☐ a moped license that's valid
- ☐ a car license that's valid
- ☐ a motorcycle license that's valid
- ☐ any of the licenses mentioned above

Question 2 - Practice Test 1

You are allowed to overtake another vehicle on its right side _____.

- ☐ when the vehicle is attempting to switch lanes
- ☐ when the vehicle intends to make a right turn
- ☐ when the vehicle intends to make a left turn
- ☐ in none of the above situations

Question 3 - Practice Test 1

The requirements for a child to be carried in a rear facing car seat in terms of age and weight are _____.

- ☐ 4 years old and weighing less than 40 pounds
- ☐ 2 years old and weighing less than 40 pounds
- ☐ 8 years old and weighing less than 60 pounds
- ☐ none of the above

Question 4 - Practice Test 1

While you are maneuvering within a roundabout, and an emergency vehicle flashing its lights approaches, you should _____.

- ☐ veer towards the center of the road, allowing the emergency vehicle to pass
- ☐ Slow your speed, pull to the right, and allow the emergency vehicle to pass
- ☐ Continue till you reach your exit, then pull over, and let the emergency vehicle pass
- ☐ Halt in the middle of the roundabout

Question 5 - Practice Test 1

On roads where traffic flows in two or more lanes in each direction, broken white lines are used _____.

- ☐ to denote the right edge of the road
- ☐ to divide the road into separate lanes for traffic moving in opposite directions
- ☐ to mark the left edge of the road
- ☐ to divide each side of the road into separate lanes for traffic moving in the same direction

Question 6 - Practice Test 1

Your high-beam headlights should be utilized in all of the following scenarios EXCEPT _____.

- ☐ in the work zones
- ☐ on roads that are unfamiliar to you
- ☐ where pedestrians might be present near the road
- ☐ in weather conditions like fog, rain, or snow

Question 7 - Practice Test 1

Your vehicle has been driven into a flooded region. Which of the following claims is/are accurate, if any?

- ☐ Maintain a greater following distance when driving through water
- ☐ If brakes are applied hard, they might lock up
- ☐ Pump your brakes after passing through the water to dry them and check their functionality
- ☐ All of the above are true

Question 8 - Practice Test 1

When a solid center line is present on your side of the road, you should

- ☐ refrain from overtaking
- ☐ change lanes
- ☐ avoid increasing your speed
- ☐ stop

Question 9 - Practice Test 1

As you reach the end of an on-ramp while merging onto a freeway, you should be traveling _____.

- ☐ as close to the speed of the traffic as possible
- ☐ at a slower speed than the rest of the traffic
- ☐ at a speed of 30 miles per hour
- ☐ at a speed of 50 miles per hour

Question 10 - Practice Test 1

Before you pull out from a parallel parking spot on the right side of the street, you should _____.

- ☐ signal a right turn and check over your right shoulder
- ☐ signal a left turn and check over your right shoulder
- ☐ signal a left turn and check over your left shoulder
- ☐ signal a right turn and check over your left shoulder

Question 11 - Practice Test 1

Which location is most likely for collisions to happen between cars and motorcycles?

- ☐ Single-lane roads
- ☐ Intersections
- ☐ Roundabouts
- ☐ Highways

Question 12 - Practice Test 1

When a vehicle makes a turn, the path of its rear wheels is _____ compared to the front wheels.

- ☐ more rapid
- ☐ longer
- ☐ slower
- ☐ shorter

Question 13 - Practice Test 1

What does a yield sign signify for a driver?

- ☐ Perform a U-turn if necessary
- ☐ Stop if there is a vehicle or pedestrian coming from a different direction
- ☐ Turn if needed
- ☐ Speed up

Question 14 - Practice Test 1

When approaching an intersection, what sequence should you follow before proceeding?

- ☐ Left-left-right rule
- ☐ Right-left-right rule
- ☐ Left-right rule
- ☐ Left-right-left rule

A double solid white line signifies what?

- ☐ Lanes going in the same direction can be crossed
- ☐ Lanes going in the same direction can't be crossed
- ☐ Lanes going in opposite directions can't be crossed
- ☐ Lanes going in opposite directions can be crossed

Which devices are used to alert drivers about construction zones or abnormal conditions ahead?

- ☐ Flashing arrow panels
- ☐ Drums
- ☐ Vertical panels
- ☐ Barricades

How far ahead should you look when driving in city traffic?

- ☐ Two blocks ahead
- ☐ One block ahead
- ☐ Three blocks ahead
- ☐ Four blocks ahead

Question 18 - Practice Test 1

What should you do when leaving a high-speed, two-lane roadway with traffic behind you?

- ☐ Increase your speed
- ☐ Apply heavy braking while maintaining steady steering
- ☐ Slow down as quickly as possible
- ☐ Do not slow down suddenly

Question 19 - Practice Test 1

Which type of alcoholic beverage is most frequently consumed by intoxicated drivers?

- ☐ Champagne
- ☐ Wine
- ☐ Beer
- ☐ Hard liquor

Question 20 - Practice Test 1

What do we call the system of ramps that connect a highway to another highway or a road?

- ☐ Entrance ramp
- ☐ Intersection
- ☐ Interchange
- ☐ Exit ramp

Question 21 - Practice Test 1

In which scenario is it NOT permissible to overtake a vehicle on the right?

- ☐ When you are in the left-turn lane
- ☐ When the vehicle you wish to pass is in the left-turn lane
- ☐ On one-way streets where all lanes are moving in the same direction
- ☐ On freeways that have at least two lanes going in the direction you are traveling

Question 22 - Practice Test 1

A "Speed Zone Ahead" sign is indicating that you're about to enter:

- ☐ An area with a maximum speed limit of 65 mph
- ☐ A freeway or expressway
- ☐ An area where the minimum speed limit is 45 mph
- ☐ An area where a slower speed limit has been established

Question 23 - Practice Test 1

On a roadway with multiple lanes heading in the same direction, which lane(s) should be used for passing other vehicles?

- ☐ The middle lanes
- ☐ The right-most lane
- ☐ Any of the lanes
- ☐ The left-most or middle lanes

Question 24 - Practice Test 1

A broad white line painted across a lane before an intersection is called a:

- ☐ Pedestrian crosswalk line
- ☐ Lane merge line
- ☐ Yield line
- ☐ Stop line

Question 25 - Practice Test 1

The area of a freeway beyond the solid white line is designated for:

- ☐ Halting only
- ☐ Parking exclusively
- ☐ Making U-turns only
- ☐ Use in emergencies only

Question 26 - Practice Test 1

If you see a pedestrian using a service animal or a white cane at an intersection, what should you do?

- ☐ Bring your vehicle to a stop
- ☐ Switch on your headlights to signal the pedestrian
- ☐ Lower your speed and pass slowly
- ☐ Use your horn to alert the pedestrian

Skidding due to locked wheels is often a result of:

- ☐ The driving wheels losing grip with the road surface
- ☐ The ignition being switched to the lock position while the vehicle is in motion
- ☐ Simultaneously pressing the accelerator and brake pedals
- ☐ Applying the brakes too forcefully at high speed

Question 28 - Practice Test 1

If another vehicle is overtaking you, you should _____ until the pass is complete.

- ☐ avoid increasing your speed
- ☐ stop your vehicle
- ☐ move towards the left
- ☐ speed up

Question 29 - Practice Test 1

If your vehicle begins to submerge into water, your course of action should be to:

- ☐ Attempt to open the door to escape
- ☐ Gradually roll down the window to prevent the vehicle from flooding
- ☐ Instantly roll down the window to exit your vehicle
- ☐ Stay inside your vehicle, dial the emergency number, and wait for assistance

Question 30 - Practice Test 1

When multiple lanes of traffic are moving in the same direction, slower-moving vehicles should ideally occupy:

- ☐ The left-most lane
- ☐ The left lane, except when passing another vehicle or making a right turn
- ☐ The middle lane
- ☐ The right-most lane, except when passing another vehicle or making a left turn

Question 31 - Practice Test 1

Which of these statements regarding right-of-way is incorrect?

- ☐ Vehicles making a left turn should yield to oncoming traffic
- ☐ At a T-intersection without control signals, vehicles on the through road should yield to those on the terminating road
- ☐ Vehicles should yield to pedestrians at unmarked crosswalks
- ☐ Vehicles entering or crossing a road from a private driveway must yield to all vehicles approaching on the road

Question 32 - Practice Test 1

If a broken yellow line is situated on your side of the center stripe, this means:

- ☐ You are not permitted to cross the line
- ☐ You may cross the line only if the opposing side also has a broken line
- ☐ You are allowed to cross the line for overtaking other vehicles
- ☐ None of the aforementioned statements apply

Question 33 - Practice Test 1

Parking lights are meant to be used when:

- ☐ Overtaking other vehicles
- ☐ During parking and reversing maneuvers
- ☐ During reversing maneuvers only
- ☐ While the vehicle is parked

Question 34 - Practice Test 1

If vehicles from a different roadway are merging onto the one you are on, what should you do?

- ☐ Disregard the merging vehicles since you have the right-of-way
- ☐ Adjust your speed and the position of your vehicle to facilitate the vehicles merging
- ☐ Honk your horn to alert the merging vehicles of your presence
- ☐ Change lanes immediately

Question 35 - Practice Test 1

If you're operating a vehicle under physical or emotional stress, it's recommended that you:

- ☐ Stop driving or have another person take over
- ☐ Drive faster to reach your destination sooner
- ☐ Consume medication
- ☐ Engage in conversation on your cell phone

Question 36 - Practice Test 1

When is it permissible to cross lowered railroad gates?

- ☐ Once you see that the train has passed
- ☐ If you're certain that no trains are approaching
- ☐ At light rail crossings
- ☐ Never

Question 37 - Practice Test 1

After overtaking a tractor-trailer, when can you safely merge back in front of the truck?

- ☐ When you can establish eye contact with the truck driver via a side mirror
- ☐ When you can view the entire front of the truck in your rear-view mirror
- ☐ When the truck honks its horn to signal that it's safe
- ☐ When you can't see the truck from your side window anymore

Question 38 - Practice Test 1

Prior to changing lanes, you should:

- ☐ Check your mirrors
- ☐ Signal your intentions
- ☐ Check your blind spots
- ☐ Perform all of the above

Question 39 - Practice Test 1

When you are driving alongside a truck going in the same direction, you should stay as far to the side as possible to prevent:

- ☐ A rear-end collision
- ☐ A sideswipe accident
- ☐ A direct hit
- ☐ A head-on collision

Question 40 - Practice Test 1

You should always decrease your speed in the following situations:

- ☐ On sharp curves
- ☐ On wet roads
- ☐ On hills
- ☐ In all the aforementioned scenarios

PRACTICE TEST 2

Gear up for the DMV driving permit test by engaging with practice questions that bear a striking resemblance (and are frequently identical!) to the ones you'll encounter on the actual DMV exam.

Total Questions: 40
Correct Answer to pass: 32

Question 1 - Practice Test 2

In the event that your vehicle breaks down on train tracks with a train approaching, what is the appropriate course of action?

- ☐ Alert the train by opening your doors and signaling
- ☐ Quickly evacuate the vehicle and move a safe distance away
- ☐ Attempt to restart the engine
- ☐ Make an effort to push the vehicle off the tracks

Question 2 - Practice Test 2

What should you do if another driver is tailgating you?

- ☐ Shift into the left lane
- ☐ Gradually decrease your speed and pull off the road if needed
- ☐ Speed up
- ☐ Brake to dissuade the tailgater

Question 3 - Practice Test 2

When double solid lines are present next to your lane, it means you are:

- ☐ Not permitted to pass or change lanes
- ☐ Permitted to pass
- ☐ Allowed to change lanes
- ☐ Allowed to make a turn

Question 4 - Practice Test 2

In heavy rain, your car's tires can lose contact with the road by riding on a layer of water. This is known as:

- ☐ Waterplaning
- ☐ Rainplaning
- ☐ Frictionplaning
- ☐ Hydroplaning

Question 5 - Practice Test 2

Typically, _____ are diamond-shaped with black letters or symbols on a yellow background.

- ☐ Warning signs
- ☐ Service signs
- ☐ Regulatory signs
- ☐ Destination signs

Question 6 - Practice Test 2

When the road is _____, you should reduce your speed by half.

☐ slippery

☐ wet

☐ packed with snow

☐ none of the above

Question 7 - Practice Test 2

When faced with an aggressive driver, you should:

☐ Engage in calling names

☐ Exit your vehicle

☐ Make rude gestures

☐ Avoid eye contact

Question 8 - Practice Test 2

In the event of a tire blowout while driving, you should:

☐ Accelerate

☐ Brake forcefully

☐ Shift to a higher gear

☐ Grip the steering wheel firmly

Question 9 - Practice Test 2

At an intersection, a solid yellow traffic light signifies that you should:

☐ Accelerate to pass the signal before it turns red

☐ Slow down and proceed with caution

☐ Maintain your current speed

☐ Prepare to stop for a red light

Question 10 - Practice Test 2

If your vehicle's rear wheels begin to skid, what should you do?

- ☐ Steer the wheel to the left
- ☐ Steer the wheel in the direction of the skid
- ☐ Steer the wheel opposite the skid
- ☐ Steer the wheel to the right

Question 11 - Practice Test 2

When two vehicles approach an intersection from opposite directions at roughly the same time, _____.

- ☐ the left-turning vehicle must yield to the vehicle going straight or turning right
- ☐ the vehicle with more passengers should go first
- ☐ the vehicle on the right must yield to the vehicle on the left
- ☐ the right-turning vehicle must yield to the left-turning vehicle

Question 12 - Practice Test 2

To maintain an appropriate space cushion between your vehicle and the one ahead, apply the:

- ☐ Three-second rule
- ☐ Two-second rule
- ☐ Four-second rule
- ☐ One-second rule

Question 13 - Practice Test 2

When entering a roundabout, rotary, or traffic circle, you must yield the right-of-way to:

☐ Pedestrians

☐ Both pedestrians and vehicles already in the circle

☐ Vehicles in the circle

☐ Nobody

Question 14 - Practice Test 2

Two-thirds of all deer-vehicle collisions occur during which of the following months?

☐ January, February, and March

☐ October, November, and December

☐ March, April, and May

☐ June, July, and August

Question 15 - Practice Test 2

For improved visibility in fog, rain, or snow, use:

☐ Emergency lights

☐ Low-beam headlights

☐ High-beam headlights

☐ Interior lights

Question 16 - Practice Test 2

You shall not pass a vehicle on the left if:

- ☐ Your lane has a broken white line
- ☐ Your lane has a solid yellow center line
- ☐ You are far away from a curve
- ☐ Your lane has a broken yellow line

Question 17 - Practice Test 2

_____ enable vehicles to exit expressways.

- ☐ Exit ramps
- ☐ Turnpikes
- ☐ Acceleration lanes
- ☐ Roundabouts

Question 18 - Practice Test 2

To perform a turnaround on a narrow, two-way street, execute:

- ☐ Single-point turn
- ☐ Two-point turn
- ☐ Four-point turn
- ☐ Three-point turn

Question 19 - Practice Test 2

Even ____ alcoholic drink(s) can impact your ability to drive safely.

- ☐ three
- ☐ four
- ☐ one
- ☐ two

Question 20 - Practice Test 2

When another vehicle passes you on the left, you should _____ until the vehicle has safely overtaken you.

☐ pull over and stop

☐ accelerate and keep to the right

☐ slow down and stay to the left

☐ slow down and stay centered in your lane

Question 21 - Practice Test 2

When turning right on a multi-lane road, which lane should you typically use?

☐ Any lane

☐ The leftmost lane

☐ A middle lane

☐ The rightmost lane

Question 22 - Practice Test 2

What should you do when an emergency vehicle with flashing lights, a siren, or an air horn is approaching you from any direction?

☐ Change lanes and maintain the same speed

☐ Pull over to the right and stop

☐ Decelerate and move into the left lane

☐ Accelerate and clear the lane

Question 23 - Practice Test 2

At a railroad crossing, what do flashing red lights, lowered crossing gates, or ringing bells indicate?

- ☐ A train has just passed
- ☐ A lane change is necessary
- ☐ You must stop at least 15 feet from the railroad tracks
- ☐ Slow down and proceed with caution

Question 24 - Practice Test 2

When is it prohibited to pass a vehicle on the right?

- ☐ When the vehicle is making a left turn
- ☐ When the vehicle is going straight
- ☐ When the vehicle is making a right turn
- ☐ When the vehicle is on a one-way road with two lanes of traffic

Question 25 - Practice Test 2

In open country at night, which headlights should you use?

- ☐ High-beam headlights
- ☐ Parking lights
- ☐ Low-beam headlights
- ☐ None of the above

Question 26 - Practice Test 2

Where can crosswalks be found?

- ☐ Only on multi-lane roads
- ☐ Regardless of whether there are crosswalk lines
- ☐ Only in residential areas
- ☐ Only where there are line markings

Question 27 - Practice Test 2

Due to their size, tractor-trailers often appear to be _____.

- ☐ moving faster
- ☐ moving backward
- ☐ moving dangerously
- ☐ moving slower

Question 28 - Practice Test 2

At which locations should you always look both ways?

- ☐ Railroad crossings
- ☐ Crosswalks
- ☐ Intersections
- ☐ All of the above

When is it necessary to signal before passing another vehicle?

- ☐ Always
- ☐ Only if there are vehicles directly behind you
- ☐ If the driver of the vehicle may be unaware of your intention to pass
- ☐ On expressways with more than two lanes

Question 30 - Practice Test 2

When is it appropriate to use your horn?

- ☐ To warn pedestrians or other drivers of potential danger
- ☐ To encourage other drivers to drive faster
- ☐ To inform another driver of their mistake
- ☐ To tell pedestrians to get off the road

Question 31 - Practice Test 2

Which factor does not influence your blood alcohol concentration (BAC)?

- ☐ Time between drinks
- ☐ Your body weight
- ☐ Time since your last drink
- ☐ Type of alcohol consumed

Question 32 - Practice Test 2

Who is responsible for ensuring a child in the vehicle you're driving is properly restrained?

☐ The vehicle owner

☐ The child

☐ Yourself

☐ The child's parents

Question 33 - Practice Test 2

If a driver's left arm is extended out the window and bent upward, this indicates they intend to _____.

☐ proceed straight

☐ slow down or stop

☐ turn right

☐ turn left

Question 34 - Practice Test 2

A flashing red light signifies _____.

☐ caution

☐ slowing down

☐ the same as a stop sign

☐ the same as a yield sign

In freezing temperatures, which areas are most likely to ice over first?

- ☐ Bridges and overpasses
- ☐ Residential streets
- ☐ Tunnels
- ☐ Gravel roads

Question 36 - Practice Test 2

When a vehicle merges onto an expressway, who has the right-of-way?

- ☐ The merging vehicle
- ☐ The fastest vehicle
- ☐ Vehicles already on the expressway
- ☐ The slowest vehicle

Question 37 - Practice Test 2

If an emergency vehicle with flashing lights or a siren approaches, you must immediately pull over and stop unless _____.

- ☐ there is adequate space in another lane for it
- ☐ you are in a hurry
- ☐ you have entered a school zone
- ☐ you are in an intersection

Question 38 - Practice Test 2

You are the third vehicle to arrive at a four-way stop at different times. Which vehicle has the right-of-way?

☐ The vehicle that is not signaling

☐ The vehicle turning right

☐ The vehicle that arrived first

☐ The vehicle to your right

Question 39 - Practice Test 2

You approach a crosswalk with a pedestrian and guide dog attempting to cross the street. What should you do?

☐ Tell the pedestrian it is safe to cross

☐ Stop and turn off your engine

☐ Wait for the pedestrian to cross the street

☐ Honk your horn to indicate it is safe to cross

Question 40 - Practice Test 2

When can you safely merge back in front of a vehicle you just passed?

☐ When the driver honks to let you in

☐ When you see the entire front bumper of the passed vehicle in your rear-view mirror

☐ When you make direct eye contact with the driver in your rearview mirror.

☐ When you can't see the passing vehicle via the window.

ROAD SIGNS

In the United States, the trend is moving towards using symbols instead of words on road signs for more effective communication. These symbols break down language barriers and facilitate immediate understanding, quickly becoming the global norm for traffic control devices.

It's imperative for all drivers to be well-versed with these traffic sign symbols to ensure the smooth functioning and safety of our transportation networks.

Don't worry, we've got your back. Our resource includes over 100 questions focused on Road Signs to help you master this vital aspect.

Total Questions: 100
Correct Answer to pass: 80

Question 1 - Road Signs

What does this image represent?

- ☐ When the way ahead is clear, passing on the left is permitted
- ☐ Passing on the right is not permitted
- ☐ Passing is prohibited in both directions
- ☐ Passing is only permitted during night

Question 2 - Road Signs

What exactly does this road sign mean?

☐   A construction zone is ahead

☐   There is a parking area ahead

☐   There is a forest zone is ahead

☐   There's a rest stop ahead

Question 3 - Road Signs

What does this image represent?

☐   A child care center

☐   T-intersection ahead

☐   Playground ahead

☐   School zone ahead

Question 4 - Road Signs

What does this sign denote?

- ☐ A side street near a railroad crossing
- ☐ A bridge
- ☐ A Truck service center
- ☐ A pedestrian underpass

Question 5 - Road Signs

This symbol denotes

- ☐ a hospital zone
- ☐ wheelchair accessibility
- ☐ a parking area for the handicapped
- ☐ a pedestrian crosswalk

41

Question 6 - Road Signs

This orange triangular reflective sign indicates

☐ a vehicle that moves in a rapid pace

☐ a vehicle transporting hazardous materials

☐ a vehicle that moves slowly

☐ a truck

Question 7 - Road Signs

Which of these signs points you in the direction of a hospital?

A B C D

☐ C

☐ B

☐ A

☐ D

Question 8 - Road Signs

What does this sign indicate?

☐   Do not accelerate to 45 mph

☐   Drive at a 45-mph speed

☐   There is a speed zone is ahead; prepare to slow down to 45 mph

☐   Construction zone ahead

Question 9 - Road Signs

Typically, a vertical rectangular traffic sign gives

☐   instructions to the driver

☐   directions to the driver to come to a halt

☐   a warning about the construction work

☐   a warning about the road's condition

Question 10 - Road Signs

This symbol denotes

☐   a lane for turning left

☐   a diversion

☐   that the road ahead curves to the left

☐   a lane for turning right

Question 11 - Road Signs

This symbol indicates

☐   railroad crossing

☐   road work

☐   a right turn

☐   road maintenance

Question 12 - Road Signs

What is the significance of this flashing arrow panel?

☐   The lane ahead of you has been closed

☐   The lane ahead is open for traffic

☐   Flaggers are in front

☐   There are right lane curves ahead

Question 13 - Road Signs

What does this sign indicate?

☐   A divided highway begins ahead

☐   One-way traffic ahead

☐   The divided highway ends ahead

☐   Merging Traffic

Question 14 - Road Signs

What is the meaning of this sign?

- ☐ When the green arrow is ON, left turns are permitted
- ☐ When the steady green signal is lit and there are no oncoming vehicles, left turns are permitted
- ☐ When the green arrow goes out, no left turns are permitted
- ☐ Left turns are only permitted when the steady green signal is OFF

Question 15 - Road Signs

What exactly does this sign mean?

- ☐ There is disabled parking ahead.
- ☐ There is a disabled crossing ahead.
- ☐ A hospital is on the way.
- ☐ There is a pedestrian crosswalk ahead.

Question 16 - Road Signs

This warning sign informs drivers that

☐ a single-use path crossing ahead

☐ there is a school zone ahead

☐ it is a bicycle lane

☐ a multi-use path crossing is ahead

Question 17 - Road Signs

This symbol indicates that

☐ bicyclists should only ride in the lane designated by the sign

☐ there is a bikeway crosses the road ahead

☐ bicyclists are not allowed to use this lane

☐ there is a no-passing zone for bicyclists ahead

Question 18 - Road Signs

If you see this sign while driving in the left lane, what should you do?

- ☐ continue straight
- ☐ merge into the right lane
- ☐ turn left
- ☐ turn right

Question 19 - Road Signs

This warning sign indicates

- ☐ there will be sharp right and left turns
- ☐ the road ahead takes a left turn
- ☐ a winding road
- ☐ that the road ahead bends to the right, then to the left

Question 20 - Road Signs

What does this signal indicate at an intersection?

- ☐ Pedestrians are not allowed to enter the crosswalk
- ☐ Drivers must slow down
- ☐ Pedestrians who are already in the crosswalk may finish their crossing
- ☐ Pedestrians are permitted to enter the crosswalk

Question 21 - Road Signs

What does this symbol indicate?

- ☐ A hospital ahead
- ☐ There is a rest stop ahead
- ☐ High school ahead
- ☐ Handicapped service

Question 22 - Road Signs

This symbol indicates

☐   the exit number 117 is up ahead

☐   next available exit is 117 miles away

☐   to enter the Route 117, take this exit

☐   none of the above

Question 23 - Road Signs

This sign indicates the location of

☐   a gas station

☐   a handicapped service

☐   a rest zone

☐   a hospital zone

Question 24 - Road Signs

What does this sign mean?

- ☐ Speed limit ahead
- ☐ Speed restriction on-ramp
- ☐ Speed advisory at roundabout
- ☐ An exit speed restriction

Question 25 - Road Signs

What exactly does this sign mean?

- ☐ Only left turns are permitted
- ☐ Traffic must merge to the right
- ☐ Traffic must merge to the left
- ☐ Only right turns are permitted

Question 26 - Road Signs

What exactly does this sign mean?

    ☐   You shouldn't take a right turn

    ☐   You must not take a left turn

    ☐   This section of the road is closed

    ☐   Do not merge

Question 27 - Road Signs

What exactly does this sign mean?

    ☐   A hospital zone

    ☐   Telephone service available ahead

    ☐   Gas station ahead

    ☐   There will be a rest zone ahead

Question 28 - Road Signs

What exactly does this sign indicate?

- ☐ You are about to approach a left turn
- ☐ You are about to approach a right turn
- ☐ A sharp U-turn
- ☐ A sharp left turn ahead

Question 29 - Road Signs

What should you do if you see this road sign?

- ☐ Exit the highway at a speed of at least 30 miles per hour
- ☐ Exit the highway at a speed of no more than 30 miles per hour
- ☐ Increase your speed to 30 mph to pass the vehicle in front of you
- ☐ Exit the freeway at a top speed of 60 mph

Question 30 - Road Signs

This pavement markings in this image indicate that

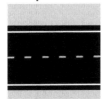

- ☐ It is not allowed to pass

- ☐ You can pass if it is safe

- ☐ Take a detour

- ☐ Make a U turn

Question 31 - Road Signs

What is the meaning of this traffic sign?

- ☐ It is not permissible to pass a vehicle on the left

- ☐ Only left turns are allowed

- ☐ Passing is legal in these directions

- ☐ Only move in the indicated directions

Question 32 - Road Signs

What does this sign mean?

☐ Hospital Zone

☐ You are approaching a A four-way intersection

☐ A side road is ahead

☐ A railroad crossing is ahead

Question 33 - Road Signs

What does this symbol indicate?

☐ Railroad crossing with low ground clearance

☐ Railroad crossing that is closed

☐ Railroad crossing that is being repaired

☐ Byway near a railroad crossing

Question 34 - Road Signs

What does this image mean?

    ☐   A broken white line that forbids passing

    ☐   A broken white line that permits passing

    ☐   An accident occurred

    ☐   The vehicle is making a U-turn

Question 35 - Road Signs

This is an octagonal (eight-sided) figure which indicates

    ☐   a Yield symbol

    ☐   Do Not Enter sign

    ☐   a Stop sign

    ☐   a Construction sign

Question 36 - Road Signs

You can find this orange sign at

- ☐ railroad crossings
- ☐ the intersections that are uncontrolled
- ☐ school zones
- ☐ work zones

Question 37 - Road Signs

What does this sign indicate?

- ☐ A winding road
- ☐ A curve ahead
- ☐ A slippery road
- ☐ A two-way road

Question 38 - Road Signs

What does this sign denote?

☐ A winding road awaits; drivers should follow the signs

☐ A gravel road ahead with sharp curves; drivers must proceed with caution

☐ When the road is wet, it becomes slippery; proceed cautiously

☐ A sharp curve near a hill; vehicles must proceed cautiously

Question 39 - Road Signs

What does this sign indicate?

☐ "Right Lane Ends"

☐ Freeway interchange

☐ Sharp turn on a highway

☐ Beginning of a Divided Highway

Question 40 - Road Signs

What does this sign indicate?

☐   You are not permitted to park on both sides of the sign

☐   You can park on the left side of the sign

☐   Parking is available to the right of the sign

☐   You are not allowed to park to the left of the sign

Question 41 - Road Signs

What does this sign mean?

☐   The divided highway ends

☐   A divided highway begins ahead

☐   There's an underpass ahead

☐   Right lane is closed

Question 42 - Road Signs

This sign means that you are

- ☐ in a wrong lane
- ☐ driving in the wrong direction
- ☐ In the city
- ☐ moving in a bicycle lane

Question 43 - Road Signs

What exactly does this sign mean?

- ☐ Take Route 45
- ☐ The top speed is 45 miles per hour any time
- ☐ The minimum speed limit is 45 miles per hour
- ☐ The maximum speed limit at night is 45 mph

Question 44 - Road Signs

What exactly does this sign indicate?

- ☐ Emergency vehicles may enter the roadway
- ☐ Trucks transporting dangerous materials may enter the road
- ☐ Heavy vehicles may enter the road
- ☐ Farm vehicles may enter the roadway

Question 45 - Road Signs

What should you do if you come across this sign at an intersection?

- ☐ Do not move further
- ☐ Continue right
- ☐ Allow oncoming traffic to pass
- ☐ Before turning right or left, yield the right-of-way or stop

Question 46 - Road Signs

What exactly does this sign indicate?

☐ At the sign, all vehicles must make a U-turn

☐ U-turns are not permitted for trucks

☐ Vehicles are not permitted to make a U-turn at the sign

☐ It denotes none of the preceding

Question 47 - Road Signs

What does this sign mean?

☐ A side road is ahead

☐ A T-intersection is ahead; yield to cross traffic

☐ A four-way stop ahead; prepare to yield

☐ A tourist information center is ahead

Question 48 - Road Signs

What exactly does this sign mean?

- ☐ A deer crossing ahead
- ☐ Cattle crossing ahead
- ☐ Forest zone
- ☐ A zoo ahead

Question 49 - Road Signs

What does this sign indicate?

- ☐ The maximum allowable speed in a school zone
- ☐ The minimum allowable speed in a school zone
- ☐ When there are children present in a school zone, this is the maximum allowable speed
- ☐ When there are children present in a school zone, this is the minimum allowable speed

Question 50 - Road Signs

What does this sign mean?

☐ Parking available

☐ Lodging available

☐ Hospital service available

☐ Handicapped service area available

Question 51 - Road Signs

What exactly does this regulatory sign mean?

☐ The indicated lane is for high-occupancy vehicles during the hours mentioned

☐ At specific times, high-occupancy vehicles are prohibited

☐ Cars and buses are not permitted during the designated times

☐ The indicated lane is only for heavy vehicles

Question 52 - Road Signs

What does a stop sign accompanied by this sign (4-way) at an intersection indicate?

☐   For four seconds, you must come to stop

☐   There are four lanes of traffic

☐   Vehicles arriving from all four directions are required to yield

☐   Vehicles approaching the intersection from all four directions must stop

Question 53 - Road Signs

What exactly does this sign denote?

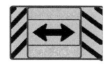

☐   The road is closed

☐   This road comes to an end at a T-intersection

☐   Narrow bridge's rails ahead

☐   A Y-intersection ahead

Question 54 - Road Signs

What does this symbol indicate?

☐   To get onto Route 47 north, make a right turn

☐   Route 47 north has one-way traffic

☐   Route 47 north begins here

☐   Route 47 comes to an end

Question 55 - Road Signs

What exactly does this sign indicate?

☐   RC flying zone ahead

☐   You're getting close to an airport

☐   Planes fly at low altitudes in that place

☐   Direction in which planes fly

Question 56 - Road Signs

What does this highway sign indicate?

☐   There is an upcoming side road

☐   There is an upcoming three-way stop

☐   There is a railroad crossing ahead

☐   There is a limited-access side road

Question 57 - Road Signs

This symbol denotes _____.

☐   a U Turn

☐   a sharp turn

☐   an emergency halt

☐   a right turn

Question 58 - Road Signs

What exactly does this sign mean?

   ☐   Speed limit on hills

   ☐   Speed limit at roundabouts

   ☐   Interstate route symbol

   ☐   A speed limit sign on expressways

Question 59 - Road Signs

What does this stop sign mean?

   ☐   Within 1,000 feet, there will be construction

   ☐   After 1,000 feet, turning right is banned

   ☐   An alternate route is 1,000 feet ahead

   ☐   There will be a parking zone ahead

Question 60 - Road Signs

What does this symbol indicate?

- ☐ A median
- ☐ There is a bump in the road ahead.
- ☐ A steep incline
- ☐ The road ahead is closed

Question 61 - Road Signs

What do this single broken (dashed) white line in the image denote?

- ☐ Traffic will be moving in the opposing directions
- ☐ Traffic moving in the same direction
- ☐ The road's shoulder
- ☐ Passing not allowed

Question 62 - Road Signs

What does this sign denote?

 ☐ School area

 ☐ Construction zone

 ☐ Road crew at work

 ☐ Pedestrian crosswalk

Question 63 - Road Signs

What does this warning sign mean?

 ☐ A stop sign ahead

 ☐ A yield sign

 ☐ Take a detour

 ☐ Slow-moving vehicles should follow directions

Question 64 - Road Signs

This sign warns drivers about

- ☐ students bus stop
- ☐ play zone for children
- ☐ school zone
- ☐ the pedestrian crosswalks

Question 65 - Road Signs

What does this regulatory sign indicate?

- ☐ Merge to the left
- ☐ Take right turn
- ☐ Do not take right turn
- ☐ Turning left is not allowed

Question 66 - Road Signs

What does the number depicted in this sign board stands for?

- ☐   A sign indicating a U.S. route marker
- ☐   An exit number
- ☐   Miles from the exit
- ☐   Speed limit on the exit ramp

Question 67 - Road Signs

This sign alerts drivers that they

- ☐   should not leave the pavement
- ☐   must extend their following distance to 6 seconds
- ☐   should move fast
- ☐   should move onto the shoulder

Question 68 - Road Signs

What exactly does this sign mean?

☐   Keep left of the divider

☐   You are getting close to a divided highway

☐   Take a detour

☐   Keep right of the divider

Question 69 - Road Signs

What exactly does this sign mean?

☐   You are not allowed to drive on the railroad tracks

☐   A railroad crossing

☐   You can drive on the railroad tracks.

☐   You must stop

Question 70 - Road Signs

What exactly does this sign mean?

- ☐ No vehicles should pass
- ☐ Slow down
- ☐ Stop for the pedestrians to cross
- ☐ Pedestrians are not allowed to cross

Question 71 - Road Signs

What do these pavement markings denote?

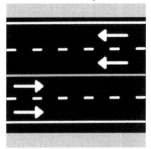

- ☐ Except for left turns, vehicles must not cross the solid yellow line
- ☐ Except for passing, vehicles must not cross the solid yellow line
- ☐ Under no circumstances may a vehicle cross the broken white lines
- ☐ None of the aforementioned

Question 72 - Road Signs

What exactly does this sign indicate?

- ☐ Stop immediately
- ☐ Pedestrian zone
- ☐ Turn right
- ☐ Flag person ahead

Question 73 - Road Signs

What does this sign indicate?

- ☐ Traffic is merging ahead
- ☐ A divided highway ahead
- ☐ Two-way road
- ☐ A narrow lane

Question 74 - Road Signs

What exactly does this sign denote?

☐ Narrow bridge ahead

☐ Acceleration lane ahead

☐ Huge traffic is ahead

☐ Narrow road ahead

Question 75 - Road Signs

What does this sign mean?

☐ The left lane comes to an end ahead

☐ The right lane comes to an end ahead

☐ A one-way road is ahead

☐ A narrow bridge ahead

Question 76 - Road Signs

You may travel in the lane indicated by this sign, _____.

- ☐   only if you're on a bicycle
- ☐   if you're passing the vehicle in front of you
- ☐   if you're on a motorcycle
- ☐   if you're transporting two or more people

Question 77 - Road Signs

What exactly is the meaning of this sign?

- ☐   There is a Y-intersection ahead
- ☐   Side road ahead.
- ☐   A hostel ahead
- ☐   Yield

Question 78 - Road Signs

What does this symbol denote?

☐   Speed limit on the interstate highway

☐   Distance between the current and the next exit

☐   The exit number

☐   Interstate highway number

Question 79 - Road Signs

This sign indicates that the parking spaces are for

☐   senior citizens

☐   bike riders

☐   the people with disabilities

☐   students

Question 80 - Road Signs

What exactly does this road sign mean?

- ☐ There is a farmhouse on the way
- ☐ A cattle crossing
- ☐ A veterinary hospital ahead
- ☐ There is a zoo ahead

Question 81 - Road Signs

What does this sign mean?

- ☐ Stopping or standing is not allowed
- ☐ A tunnel awaits you ahead
- ☐ It is not permitted to hitchhike
- ☐ You're almost to a school zone

Question 82 - Road Signs

What does this sign denote?

☐   The maximum number of vehicles that can park

☐   The maximum speed allowed on a road.

☐   A stopping place

☐   A sign indicating a United States route marking

Question 83 - Road Signs

What does this figure denote?

☐   A flag person is ahead

☐   Road crew is on the job

☐   There is a pedestrian crossing ahead; vehicles must yield.

☐   A school crossing is ahead; vehicles must move slowly

Question 84 - Road Signs

The availability of_____ is represented by this blue sign.

☐   Food

☐   Rest Area

☐   Gas station

☐   Hospital

Question 85 - Road Signs

If you see this sign and are travelling slower than the majority of traffic, what should you do?

☐   Increase your speed

☐   Enter the left lane

☐   Move to the right lane

☐   Take the next exit

Question 86 - Road Signs

What does the arrow on this sign indicate?

☐ Drivers can choose to proceed in either way

☐ Traffic must only travel in the direction indicated by the arrow

☐ The lane ahead is reserved for right-turning trucks

☐ All cars must come to a complete stop before making a right turn

Question 87 - Road Signs

What exactly does this sign mean?

☐ A left turn is ahead of you

☐ It is not permissible to turn left

☐ You will encounter a sequence of curves ahead

☐ There is a side road is entering from the right

Question 88 - Road Signs

What do these two arrows represent?

- ☐ Divided highway starts
- ☐ Divided highway ends
- ☐ Two-way traffic ahead
- ☐ Traffic may flow on both sides

Question 89 - Road Signs

What does this symbol indicate?

- ☐ Vehicles must go at a minimum of 40 miles per hour
- ☐ Slow-moving vehicles are not permitted to travel faster than 40 mph
- ☐ Vehicles should not exceed the posted speed restriction of 40 mph
- ☐ Vehicles must go at no more than 40 miles per hour

Question 90 - Road Signs

What exactly does this sign indicate?

☐   A work zone will be ahead of you

☐   There will be a bend on the way

☐   The road ahead will have a low point

☐   There will be a diversion ahead

Question 91 - Road Signs

For what purpose is this symbol used for?

☐   indicating the presence of a hospital

☐   displaying alternate routes in the event of road closures or construction

☐   Showing the designated routes

☐   Showing tourist routes

Question 92 - Road Signs

Which of the following pavement markings separates two lanes of traffic travelling in the same direction?

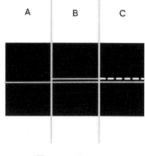

☐ B

☐ A

☐ C

☐ None of the preceding

Question 93 - Road Signs

What does this sign mean?

☐ Take neither a left nor a straight path

☐ Keep going straight

☐ Merge to the left

☐ Turn left or keep going straight

Question 94 - Road Signs

What exactly does this sign mean?

☐   Road permanently closed

☐   Handicapped Parking

☐   Parking is not permitted

☐   No U-turns

Question 95 - Road Signs

What exactly does this sign indicate?

☐   Change lanes

☐   Proceed straight

☐   Stop

☐   Take Left

Question 96 - Road Signs

What exactly do these yellow pavement markings indicate?

- ☐ Three-way intersection
- ☐ Right turns are permitted for vehicles travelling in either direction
- ☐ Left turns are permitted for vehicles travelling in either direction
- ☐ One-way street

Question 97 - Road Signs

What symbol is this?

- ☐ A stop sign
- ☐ A yield symbol
- ☐ Do Not Enter
- ☐ Work zone

Question 98 - Road Signs

What exactly does this sign mean?

- ☐ This lane permits you to turn left
- ☐ From this lane, you must make a U-turn
- ☐ You must detour at the intersection
- ☐ You have the option of making a U-turn from this lane

Question 99 - Road Signs

What does this sign mean?

- ☐ Getting close to exit 444
- ☐ You're 444 miles from the state line and the end of the road
- ☐ Arrived at Route 444
- ☐ None of the preceding

What does this signal indicate?

☐   You've arrived at an abandoned railroad track.

☐   You've arrived at a railroad crossing.

☐   There is a railroad track parallel to the road ahead.

☐   You've arrived at a train station.

SITUATIONS AND SIGNS

Presented here is a comprehensive assortment of Signage and Scenarios specifically designed to enhance your understanding of intersections and shared lanes. This collection is not just an assortment of random signs and situations but a carefully curated set of content meant to address all possible scenarios you may encounter on the road.

Total Questions: 25
Correct Answer to pass: 20

Question 1 - Signs and Situations

You notice a yellow "X" light flashing above your lane. What does it imply?

☐   You should exit this lane as soon as possible

☐   This lane is now closed

☐   This lane is clear

☐   This lane is only for turning left

Question 2 - Signs and Situations

You've come to halt 20 feet behind a school bus with flashing red lights. When will you be able to pass it?

☐   When it begins to move

☐   If a traffic officer waves you through

☐   If the bus driver waves you through

☐   All of the above

Question 3 - Signs and Situations

You notice a lane with white diamonds painted on it. What do they imply?

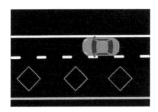

☐   This is a bus only lane

☐   This is a stop lane for emergencies

☐   This lane is now closed

☐   This is a reserved lane

Question 4 - Signs and Situations

At around the same moment, two cars arrive at an intersection. Which of the following statements is correct?

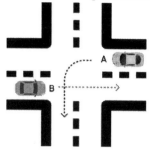

☐ All vehicles turning left must yield to Car B

☐ The drivers must select who will drive first

☐ Car A must yield since it is making a left turn

☐ None of the preceding statements are correct

Question 5 - Signs and Situations

You've parked facing a steep downhill slope. Which of the following actions should you take?

☐ If you have a manual transmission, keep it in reverse

☐ If you have a manual transmission, keep it in first gear

☐ If you have an automatic transmission, keep it in first gear

☐ If you have an automatic transmission, keep it in reverse

Question 6 - Signs and Situations

Three vehicles reach an intersection simultaneously. Who has the right-of-way?

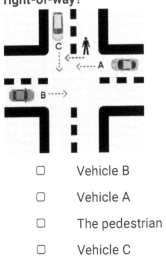

- ☐ Vehicle B
- ☐ Vehicle A
- ☐ The pedestrian
- ☐ Vehicle C

Question 7 - Signs and Situations

An emergency vehicle with flashing lights is stopped up ahead. What should you do?

- ☐ Accelerate and pass the emergency vehicle as quickly as possible
- ☐ Slow down; also, change to a non-adjacent lane if possible
- ☐ Change to a non-adjacent lane if possible; otherwise, slow down
- ☐ Proceed with the same pace

Question 8 - Signs and Situations

You have parked uphill on a steep incline. What should you do?

- ☐ Set your automatic transmission to first gear
- ☐ Set your automatic transmission to reverse
- ☐ Set your manual transmission to first gear
- ☐ Set your manual transmission to reverse

Question 9 - Signs and Situations

Which of the following takes priority (i.e., should be obeyed above all the others)?

- ☐ A red traffic light
- ☐ A traffic officer
- ☐ A stopped school bus with flashing red lights
- ☐ A warning road sign

Question 10 - Signs and Situations

What should you do when you see a flashing red light?

- ☐ You are not required to stop or yield at a flashing red signal
- ☐ When it is safe to do so, stop, yield, and then proceed
- ☐ Proceed with caution because the traffic signal is out
- ☐ Stop and hold your breath until the light turns green

Question 11 - Signs and Situations

You approach a railroad crossing with flashing red lights and a signal bell. A train is visible. Which of the following is correct?

☐ (a) You must stop at least 15 feet from the tracks

☐ (b) You can cross the tracks as soon as the train passed

☐ Both (a) and (b) are correct

☐ Neither (a) nor (b) is correct

Question 12 - Signs and Situations

You approach an intersection and notice a certain sign. What are your options?

☐ Stop completely and yield to traffic before proceeding

☐ Stop completely and then proceed

☐ Find another route; you cannot proceed through here

☐ Slow down and only proceed if the intersection is clear

Question 13 - Signs and Situations

When can you drive in a lane with this sign?

- ☐ When there is at least one passenger

- ☐ Whenever you want

- ☐ When at least two passengers are aboard

- ☐ Never (this is a bus and truck lane)

Question 14 - Signs and Situations

At at the same moment, two cars arrive at an uncontrolled intersection (one that is not controlled by signs or signals). Which of the following statements is correct?

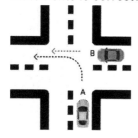

- ☐ Car A must yield because it is to the left of Car B

- ☐ Car B must yield because it is traveling straight through the intersection

- ☐ Car B must yield because it is on Car A's right

- ☐ None of the preceding statements are correct

Question 15 - Signs and Situations

You approach a crossroad with a green light and wish to drive straight through the intersection. Which of the following is correct?

☐   You are unable to proceed

☐   You are free to continue

☐   You may proceed, but you must first yield to any vehicles already present in the crossroads

☐   You must temporarily stop and cede before proceeding

Question 16 - Signs and Situations

Car B enters an intersection intending to turn right on a red light, while Car A has a green light and wants to proceed straight through the intersection. Which statement is accurate?

☐   Car A should yield to Car B

☐   Car A must accelerate to pass Car B

☐   Car B should stop and allow Car A to pass

☐   None of these options are correct

Question 17 - Signs and Situations

Before turning left into a driveway, to whom must you yield?

- ☐ Approaching vehicles
- ☐ Pedestrians
- ☐ Both pedestrians and oncoming vehicles
- ☐ No one (you have the right-of-way)

Question 18 - Signs and Situations

You're following a school bus when its yellow lights begin to flash. What does this indicate?

- ☐ The bus is signaling for you to pass safely
- ☐ The bus is preparing to stop for passengers; slow down and be ready to stop
- ☐ The bus is about to pull over, allowing you to continue at your normal speed
- ☐ The bus is stopping for passengers; you must stop immediately

Question 19 - Signs and Situations

You approach an intersection with a STOP sign. Where are you required to stop?

- ☐ Before entering the intersection
- ☐ In front of the stop line
- ☐ Prior to the crosswalk
- ☐ All of the above options apply

Question 20 - Signs and Situations

You arrive at a crossroads wanting to turn left with a green light. Can you proceed?

- ☐ Sure, but only if a Left Turn Permitted sign is present
- ☐ Sure, but first yield to pedestrians and oncoming traffic
- ☐ No, you may only turn left on a green arrow
- ☐ Sure, this is a "protected" turn, and you have the right-of-way

Question 21 - Signs and Situations

You have parked uphill next to a curb. In which direction should you point your front wheels?

- ☐ Away from the curb
- ☐ In any direction
- ☐ Towards the curb
- ☐ Straight

Question 22 - Signs and Situations

You are driving in the right lane of a four-lane highway and see a stopped emergency vehicle with its lights flashing ahead. What should you do?

- ☐ Stop in a non-adjacent lane
- ☐ Move to a non-adjacent lane if possible; otherwise, slow down
- ☐ Proceed carefully
- ☐ Stop immediately

Question 23 - Signs and Situations

The driver is using a hand signal. He/She intends to:

☐ Turn left

☐ Stop

☐ Turn right

☐ Accelerate

Question 24 - Signs and Situations

You notice an emergency vehicle approaching with its flashing lights on. What should you do?

☐ Pull over and stop, regardless of the direction the emergency vehicle is traveling

☐ Continue your journey

☐ Pull over and stop only if the emergency vehicle is traveling in your same direction

☐ Pull over and stop only if the emergency vehicle is traveling in your opposite direction

Question 25 - Signs and Situations

You are about to make a turn at an intersection, and you don't see any other vehicles nearby. Are you still required to signal?

☐ Yes, signal for at least 500 feet.

☐ Yes, signal for at least 300 feet.

☐ Never

☐ Yes, signal for at least 100 feet

FINES & LIMITS

This particular segment is tailored to the laws of your State, featuring 10 questions focused on Fines and Limits. It is known to be one of the most challenging sections, often being the stumbling block for many test-takers.

Total Questions: 10
Correct Answer to pass: 8

Question 1 - Fines & Limits

You can't leave the vehicle unattended on a road with limited access for more than _____ hours.

- ☐ 4
- ☐ 10
- ☐ 12
- ☐ 24

Question 2 - Fines & Limits

Which of the following fees must you pay if you are found guilty of DUI for the first time?

- ☐ $100 to the Alcohol Education and Rehabilitation Fund (AERF)
- ☐ $75 to Safe Neighborhood Services
- ☐ $100 to the fund for drunk driving
- ☐ the entire list above

Question 3 - Fines & Limits

You will be compelled to perform ___ days of community service if you are convicted of drinking and driving twice.

- ☐ 20
- ☐ 10
- ☐ 30
- ☐ 60

Question 4 - Fines & Limits

If you are found guilty of driving through a safety zone, your driving record will be added with ___ points.

- ☐ 5
- ☐ 4
- ☐ 2
- ☐ 6

Question 5 - Fines & Limits

You will receive ___ points on your driving record if you are found guilty of driving on a sidewalk.

- ☐ 5
- ☐ 4
- ☐ 3
- ☐ 2

Question 6 - Fines & Limits

Which of the following will aid a drunk driver in sobering up?

- ☐ An icy shower
- ☐ The passage of time
- ☐ A large meal
- ☐ Coffee

Question 7 - Fines & Limits

If you are found guilty of DUI and it was your first offense, you might receive a sentence of up to _____ days in jail.

- ☐ 30
- ☐ 15
- ☐ 45
- ☐ 60

Question 8 - Fines & Limits

If it was your first violation and you are found guilty of operating a vehicle without liability insurance, your license will be suspended for _____.

- ☐ 1 year
- ☐ 2 years
- ☐ 6 months
- ☐ 2 months

Question 9 - Fines & Limits

Installing an ignition interlock device (IID) for at least _____ is required if you are convicted of DUI for the first time.

- ☐ 12 months
- ☐ 9 months
- ☐ 3 months
- ☐ 6 months

Question 10 - Fines & Limits

If it was your first offense and you were found guilty of reckless driving, you may receive a sentence of _____ days in jail.

- ☐ 120
- ☐ 45
- ☐ 90
- ☐ 60

DISTRACTED DRIVING TEST

This section is of paramount importance. It will probe your understanding of contemporary driving distractions, along with the implications of driving under the influence of drugs and medication.

Total Questions: 20
Correct Answer to pass: 16

Question 1 - Distracted Driving

Which of the following statements about cell phones is accurate?

☐ It is quicker to make a call while driving

☐ The use of a hands-free cell phone while driving is permitted for adults

☐ Cell phones can be used while driving for adults

☐ If you get a call while you're driving, you should slow down before answering

Question 2 - Distracted Driving

Something happening in the backseat requires your attention while you are driving. What should you do?

☐ As you continue to drive, slow down and handle the issue

☐ Turn around and cope with the situation, occasionally looking ahead

☐ Before addressing the issue, pull over to the side of the road and park your vehicle

☐ You should adjust the rearview mirror to see the back seat

Question 3 - Distracted Driving

What should you do before driving if you feel sleepy?

- ☐ Sleep
- ☐ Music-listening
- ☐ consume coffee
- ☐ Exercise

Question 4 - Distracted Driving

What medications, excluding alcohol, can impair one's capacity for safe driving?

- ☐ Prescription drugs
- ☐ Non-prescription medications
- ☐ Medications used to treat migraines, colds, hay fever, various allergies, or to soothe the nerves
- ☐ The entire list above

Question 5 - Distracted Driving

Is it safe to take medications before driving?

- ☐ Only with a valid prescription
- ☐ No
- ☐ Only if the physician states that it won't impair safe driving
- ☐ Only over-the-counter versions

Question 6 - Distracted Driving

It's _____ to text and drive.

- ☐ legal
- ☐ legal if you do not exceed 15 mph
- ☐ legal only when you stop at a STOP sign
- ☐ illegal

Question 7 - Distracted Driving

Talking on a cell phone while driving increases the likelihood of a collision _____.

- ☐ up to four times
- ☐ up to three times
- ☐ by some more amount
- ☐ at least twice

Question 8 - Distracted Driving

Is it legal for teenage drivers to talk on their cell phones while driving?

- ☐ Only when traveling at less than 25 mph
- ☐ Only if you're on a country road
- ☐ Yes, as long as you're cautious
- ☐ It is illegal to use a cell phone while driving

Question 9 - Distracted Driving

To avoid being a distracted driver, you should:

- ☐ smoke, eat, and drink only on straight sections of the road
- ☐ consult maps or use your phone when no other vehicles are around you
- ☐ have all emotionally challenging conversations during your initial hour of driving
- ☐ switch off your cell phone until you arrive at your destination

Question 10 - Distracted Driving

Fatigue can impact your driving by:

- ☐ Compromising your judgement
- ☐ Slowing down your reaction times
- ☐ Reducing your awareness
- ☐ All of the above

Question 11 - Distracted Driving

Potential distractions while driving include:

- ☐ Constantly checking mirrors
- ☐ Checking blind spots
- ☐ Frequently checking the traffic behind you
- ☐ Text messaging and talking on the phone

Question 12 - Distracted Driving

Which types of drugs can influence your ability to safely operate a vehicle?

- ☐ Over-the-counter drugs
- ☐ Prescription drugs
- ☐ Illegal drugs
- ☐ All of the above mentioned

Question 13 - Distracted Driving

To combat highway hypnosis, drowsiness, and fatigue, drivers should _____ to stay awake while driving.

- ☐ Take stimulants
- ☐ Do exercise their eyes
- ☐ Text message their loved ones
- ☐ Talk on a cell phone

Question 14 - Distracted Driving

Which of the following activities will not negatively affect your driving on the road?

- ☐ Eating
- ☐ Smoking
- ☐ Drinking coffee
- ☐ Listening to the radio

Question 15 - Distracted Driving

A minor driver receives a phone call on their cell phone. He/she should:

- ☐   not carry a cell phone while driving
- ☐   not answer the call
- ☐   use a hands-free cell phone to answer the call
- ☐   answer the call only in an emergency

Question 16 - Distracted Driving

Which of the following actions will NOT help prevent distracted driving?

- ☐   Preprogramming your favorite radio stations
- ☐   Adjusting all your mirrors before starting
- ☐   Pre-loosening the coffee cup lid
- ☐   Preplanning the route

Question 17 - Distracted Driving

Which of the following actions is NOT a safe driving practice?

- ☐   Texting and operating visual screen devices while driving
- ☐   Looking forward and sideways while parking
- ☐   Using side mirrors while you drive
- ☐   Humming to music while you drive

Question 18 - Distracted Driving

Be aware of the following potential distractions or impairments while driving:

- ☐ Alcohol, drugs, and certain medications
- ☐ Adjusting electronic controls and vehicle features
- ☐ Listening to loud music, using devices such as cell phones, GPS, and intercoms
- ☐ All of the above mentioned

Question 19 - Distracted Driving

Which statement is accurate?

- ☐ Sending and reading short texts while driving is acceptable
- ☐ If you are lost, you can quickly input navigation instructions while driving
- ☐ Having lunch while driving is safe and time-efficient
- ☐ It is legal to use audio navigation while driving

Question 20 - Distracted Driving

Is it safe to hold something in your lap while driving?

- ☐ Yes, as long as it's not a human or a pet
- ☐ Yes, if it's a small animal
- ☐ Yes, as long as you don't get distracted
- ☐ No way, Never

DRINKING AND DRIVING TEST

This segment delves into the repercussions of driving under the influence of alcohol. It's essential to grasp the restrictions associated with alcohol consumption and its impact on your physical condition while driving.

Total Questions: 20
Correct Answer to pass: 16

Question 1 - Drinking and Driving

What can lead to the suspension of your driving privilege?

- ☐ Having an unopened, sealed container of alcohol in your vehicle
- ☐ Declining to choose a designated sober driver
- ☐ Carrying closed containers of alcohol while working for someone with an off-site liquor sales license
- ☐ Refusing to take a blood and/or urine test

Question 2 - Drinking and Driving

What can help an intoxicated person sober up?

- ☐ Time
- ☐ A cup of coffee
- ☐ Cold and fresh air
- ☐ All of the above

Question 3 - Drinking and Driving

What are the potential penalties for being convicted of driving under the influence of alcohol or drugs?

- ☐ License suspension
- ☐ Substantial fines and higher insurance rates
- ☐ Community service
- ☐ Any or all of the above

Question 4 - Drinking and Driving

Which is NOT a consequence of consuming alcohol?

- ☐ Increased alertness
- ☐ Slow reactions
- ☐ Impaired judgment
- ☐ Hindered vision

Question 5 - Drinking and Driving

Which of the following beverages has a standard 1.5-ounce amount of alcohol?

- ☐ A 5-ounce glass of wine
- ☐ One can of beer
- ☐ One shot of 80-proof liquor
- ☐ Each of the above

Question 6 - Drinking and Driving

Why is consuming alcohol and driving at night particularly dangerous?

- ☐ Alcohol impairs judgment more at night
- ☐ There's a higher chance of encountering drunk drivers
- ☐ Vision is already restricted
- ☐ Roads are busier at night

Question 7 - Drinking and Driving

Which factor does not impact blood alcohol concentration?

- ☐ Time during which alcohol was consumed
- ☐ Body weight
- ☐ Time since the last drink
- ☐ Alcohol type

Question 8 - Drinking and Driving

How does alcohol consumption impact driving ability?

- ☐ Reduces driving skills
- ☐ Negatively affects depth perception
- ☐ Slows down reflexes
- ☐ All of the above

Question 9 - Drinking and Driving

Which of the following actions will result in the mandatory suspension of a minor's license?

- ☐   Driving when impaired by drugs
- ☐   Transporting an open beer container
- ☐   Transporting an open liquor container
- ☐   Any or all of the preceding

Question 10 - Drinking and Driving

What is the leading cause of death for Americans aged 16 to 24?

- ☐   Kidney problems
- ☐   Drunk driving
- ☐   Drug overdose
- ☐   Cancer

Question 11 - Drinking and Driving

It is prohibited to have open containers of alcohol in a vehicle in which of the following places?

- ☐   The driver's seat
- ☐   The console
- ☐   beneath the seat
- ☐   In all of the preceding

Question 12 - Drinking and Driving

Alcohol can have an impact on your:

- ☐ Reaction time
- ☐ Judgment
- ☐ Concentration
- ☐ All of the answers given above are correct.

Question 13 - Drinking and Driving

Drinking and driving can _____.

- ☐ Impair your reflexes
- ☐ Reduce physical control over a vehicle
- ☐ Decrease a driver's awareness of road hazards
- ☐ All of the above

Question 14 - Drinking and Driving

Which of the following statements about drivers under the age of twenty-one is correct?

- ☐ They are not permitted to purchase, drink, or possess alcohol
- ☐ They are permitted to consume limited amounts of alcohol, but not while driving
- ☐ They can buy alcohol but not consume it. They can have trace levels of alcohol in their blood while driving
- ☐ They are allowed to have trace amounts of alcohol in their blood while driving

Question 15 - Drinking and Driving

After consuming a significant amount of alcohol, you can ensure you will not be driving under the influence by:

- ☐ Waiting a day or two
- ☐ Drinking only beer or wine, not hard liquor
- ☐ Waiting at least an hour
- ☐ Waiting at least 30 minutes

Question 16 - Drinking and Driving

Which of the following regions does NOT allow open containers of alcohol?

- ☐ Passenger areas of standard passenger cars
- ☐ Limousine passenger compartments
- ☐ In a passenger car's trunk
- ☐ Motorhome residential areas

Question 17 - Drinking and Driving

Which of the following is not an acceptable substitute for drinking and driving?

- ☐ Public transportation
- ☐ A designated driver
- ☐ A taxi
- ☐ Any of the preceding

Question 18 - Drinking and Driving

A driver who has consumed alcohol is more likely to _____.

☐ fail to dim headlights for oncoming traffic

☐ drive too fast or too slowly

☐ change lanes frequently

☐ do all of the preceding tasks

Question 19 - Drinking and Driving

Which of the following activities is illegal for minors?

☐ Attempting to buy alcohol

☐ Having a blood alcohol concentration (BAC) of 0.02% or higher

☐ Alcohol consumption

☐ All of the preceding

Question 20 - Drinking and Driving

As a driver's blood alcohol concentration (BAC) increases, which of the following occurs?

☐ Alcohol impairs coordination and muscle control

☐ Alcohol has a growing impact on the brain of the drinker

☐ The first processes to be impacted are self-control and judgment

☐ All of the aforementioned

EXAM TEST PRACTICE

Here is the final part of this book. Sit back, relax, and focus. This practice test has the same number of questions as your official DMV exam.

Total Questions: 50
Correct Answer to pass: 40

Question 1 - Mock Exam

On one-way roads and divided highways, what are solid yellow lines used as?

☐   Lines indicating the left edge

☐   Lines indicating the right edge

☐   Stop lines

☐   Center lines

Question 2 - Mock Exam

In construction zones, what are the typical speed limits?

☐   Increased speed limits

☐   Decreased speed limits

☐   A universal speed limit of 15 mph

☐   There are no speed limits

Question 3 - Mock Exam

In New Jersey, what is the minimum distance from a fire hydrant at which you may park?

- ☐   7 feet
- ☐   5 feet
- ☐   10 feet
- ☐   12 feet

Question 4 - Mock Exam

If you see a bus in the lane on your right about to make a right turn, what is correct?

- ☐   Buses are forbidden from making right turns
- ☐   The bus might need to shift into the left lane to execute the right turn
- ☐   The bus will turn at a slower pace compared to other vehicles
- ☐   Buses are only permitted to make turns from the right lane.

Question 5 - Mock Exam

Which of the following can impair a driver's ability to drive safely?

- ☐   Illegal drugs
- ☐   Over-the-counter cold medications
- ☐   Pep pills
- ☐   All of the above

Question 6 - Mock Exam

When there are two or more lanes of traffic moving in the same direction, which lane should slower vehicles use?

- ☐ The center lane
- ☐ The right lane, except when passing or turning left
- ☐ Any lane with the least traffic
- ☐ The left lane, except when passing or turning right

Question 7 - Mock Exam

On a potentially slippery road, if you have to stop quickly, should you pump your brakes?

- ☐ Only if your vehicle does not have anti-lock brakes (ABS)
- ☐ Only if your vehicle is equipped with anti-lock brakes (ABS)
- ☐ Yes
- ☐ Only if there are no other vehicles on the road

Question 8 - Mock Exam

A driver in front of you has his arm out of the window, pointing downward. What does this driver intend to do?

- ☐ Make a U-turn
- ☐ Turn right
- ☐ Slow down or stop
- ☐ Turn left

Question 9 - Mock Exam

If you approach a school bus with flashing red lights that has stopped on the opposite side of a divided highway, are you required to stop?

☐ Yes, you must stop until the flashing red lights are switched off

☐ Yes, but you can proceed when it's safe

☐ No, but you must reduce speed to 10 mph as you pass the school bus

☐ No, continue as usual

Question 10 - Mock Exam

What is the top speed limit on rural roads?

☐ 20 mph

☐ 30 mph

☐ 40 mph

☐ 50 mph

Question 11 - Mock Exam

You can't park within how many feet of a crosswalk at an intersection in New Jersey?

☐ 50

☐ 30

☐ 20

☐ 25

Question 12 - Mock Exam

At a four-way stop, which vehicle gets to move forward first?

- ☐   The one that reached first
- ☐   The one on the right
- ☐   The one on the left
- ☐   The one going straight through the intersection

Question 13 - Mock Exam

When multiple vehicles approach an intersection without traffic controls simultaneously, who has the right of way?

- ☐   Any vehicle that's turning
- ☐   The vehicle on your left
- ☐   All bicycles
- ☐   The vehicle on your right

Question 14 - Mock Exam

How can you communicate your intentions to other drivers?

- ☐   By signaling or using the horn
- ☐   By rolling down your window and speaking to them
- ☐   By signaling only
- ☐   By waving

During a green light, you're turning right and see a pedestrian in the crosswalk crossing the street. Who has the right-of-way?

- ☐ Your vehicle, because the light is green
- ☐ The first one who entered the intersection
- ☐ The pedestrian, because they're in a crosswalk
- ☐ Your vehicle, because you're turning right

Question 16 - Mock Exam

In a weave lane, which vehicle has the right-of-way?

- ☐ The one entering the freeway
- ☐ The faster vehicle
- ☐ The one exiting the freeway
- ☐ None of the above

Question 17 - Mock Exam

In New Jersey, can you make a right turn at a red light?

- ☐ Yes, but only if there's a sign allowing it
- ☐ Yes, this is a "protected" turn, so you have the right of way
- ☐ Yes, but only after stopping and yielding to traffic and pedestrians
- ☐ No, right turns on red are not allowed in New Jersey

Question 18 - Mock Exam

Before entering an intersection, what should you look out for?

☐ Pedestrians crossing

☐ Vehicles approaching from the left

☐ Vehicles approaching from the right

☐ All of the above

Question 19 - Mock Exam

What is the safe way to handle trucks' rear blind spots or "No-Zones"?

☐ Don't follow a truck too closely or get sandwiched between trucks

☐ Leave more space for a truck making a wide turn

☐ Stay well back from a truck that's about to reverse or is reversing

☐ All of the above

Question 20 - Mock Exam

An emergency vehicle with sirens and flashing lights is coming up behind you. What should you do?

☐ Slow down

☐ Keep moving at the same speed

☐ Pull over to the far right of the road, stop and wait for the emergency vehicle to pass

☐ Stop in your lane and wait for the emergency vehicle to pass

Question 21 - Mock Exam

When is it permissible to use studded snow tires in New Jersey?

- ☐ Between April 1 and November 15
- ☐ Between November 15 and April 1
- ☐ Between April 15 and November 1
- ☐ Between November 1 and April 15

Question 22 - Mock Exam

What should you do if you begin to skid on a slick road?

- ☐ Keep the front wheels straight and remove your foot from the gas pedal
- ☐ Steer the front wheels towards the skid and let off the gas pedal
- ☐ Steer the front wheels to the right and press on the gas pedal
- ☐ Steer the front wheels towards the skid and press on the gas pedal

Question 23 - Mock Exam

What should you do after driving through a deep puddle?

- ☐ Accelerate
- ☐ Stop and allow your brakes to dry
- ☐ Pump your brakes
- ☐ Perform all of the above actions

Question 24 - Mock Exam

If your windshield wipers fail during rain or snow, what should you do?

- ☐ Brake hard and exit the road
- ☐ Lower the driver's side window and extend your head out to see ahead
- ☐ Decelerate and exit the road
- ☐ Perform all of the above actions

Question 25 - Mock Exam

What do you mean by a No-Zone?

- ☐ An area where parking is not allowed
- ☐ A large vehicle's blind spot
- ☐ A school zone
- ☐ A highway work zone

Question 26 - Mock Exam

If the road is slippery, in which direction might your vehicle skid while navigating a curve?

- ☐ To the right
- ☐ To the left
- ☐ In a straight line
- ☐ Backwards

Question 27 - Mock Exam

If you possess a basic driver's license, are you permitted to use a cell phone while driving?

- ☐ Yes, but only on rural roads
- ☐ Yes, but only with a hands-free device
- ☐ No, never
- ☐ Yes, if you exercise caution

Question 28 - Mock Exam

When leaving a highway, what should you do?

- ☐ Begin slowing down while still on the highway
- ☐ Begin slowing down once you've entered the deceleration lane
- ☐ Accelerate before the exit
- ☐ Start to speed up once you're in the deceleration lane

Question 29 - Mock Exam

If a vehicle is tailgating you, what should you do?

- ☐ Increase your speed to elude the driver behind you
- ☐ Beep your horn to alert the driver
- ☐ Stop your vehicle on the road and argue with the driver
- ☐ Decelerate and encourage the driver behind you to overtake

Question 30 - Mock Exam

When is it permissible to make a left turn from the middle lane of a multi-lane roadway?

- ☐ When traffic prevents you from merging into the left lane
- ☐ When you're turning from a one-way road
- ☐ When signs, signals, or pavement markings allow it
- ☐ When you're turning onto a one-way road

Question 31 - Mock Exam

When driving on a highway with a speed limit of 65 mph, while most traffic is moving at 70 mph, how fast should you be driving?

- ☐ 65 mph
- ☐ 60 mph
- ☐ 70 mph
- ☐ 75 mph

Question 32 - Mock Exam

When there's both a solid yellow line and a dashed yellow line separating opposite lanes, you are NOT permitted to overtake _____.

- ☐ if the dashed yellow line is on your side
- ☐ if the solid yellow line is on your side
- ☐ if the solid yellow line isn't on your side
- ☐ under any circumstances

Question 33 - Mock Exam

White diamond symbols painted on a lane signify that the lane is a:

- ☐ Turn lane
- ☐ Passing lane
- ☐ High-occupancy vehicle (HOV) lane
- ☐ Exit ramp

Question 34 - Mock Exam

Which statement about railroad crossings is incorrect?

- ☐ It's advisable to check for more than one track before crossing
- ☐ You should never start crossing if there's no room for your vehicle on the other side
- ☐ Shifting gears while crossing railroad tracks is a good practice
- ☐ Vehicles must yield to crossing trains

Question 35 - Mock Exam

A double solid yellow line separates two lanes of traffic that are:

- ☐ Moving in opposite directions
- ☐ Moving in the same direction
- ☐ Merging to the right
- ☐ Merging to the left

Question 36 - Mock Exam

You should maintain a steady speed when passing and reentering the lane in front of trucks or buses because they require:

- ☐ More distance to slow down compared to cars
- ☐ Less distance to slow down compared to cars
- ☐ Less time to stop compared to cars
- ☐ Less space to maneuver compared to cars

Question 37 - Mock Exam

If it begins raining on a hot day, caution is necessary as the pavement may become slippery. This is caused by:

- ☐ Oil in the vehicle
- ☐ Water in the asphalt
- ☐ Melting tires
- ☐ Oil in the asphalt

Question 38 - Mock Exam

When changing lanes, all of the following are appropriate actions EXCEPT _____.

- ☐ Checking your rear-view and side mirrors
- ☐ Checking your blind spots by looking over your shoulder in the direction you intend to move
- ☐ Not taking your eyes off the road ahead for more than a moment
- ☐ Turning the steering wheel when you turn your head to check your blind spots

Question 39 - Mock Exam

When driving on a two-way road without centerline markings, what should you do?

☐ Always drive on the left

☐ Leave at least half the road for vehicles moving in the opposite direction

☐ Use the full road when there's no oncoming traffic

☐ None of the above

Question 40 - Mock Exam

Consuming two to four alcoholic drinks will impair which of the following?

☐ Reaction time

☐ Coordination

☐ Vision

☐ All of the above

Question 41 - Mock Exam

What type of line indicates the outer edge of a roadway and can only be crossed by traffic moving to or from the shoulder?

☐ broken yellow line

☐ solid white line

☐ solid yellow line

☐ broken white line

If you are driving at 50 mph on dry pavement, approximately how far will it take you to stop?

- ☐   50 feet
- ☐   125 feet
- ☐   200 feet
- ☐   247 feet

Question 43 - Mock Exam

How can a highway work zone be easily identified?

- ☐   a pentagonal (five-sided) yellow-green sign
- ☐   an octagonal (eight-sided) red sign
- ☐   a pennant-shaped yellow sign
- ☐   a rectangular or diamond-shaped orange sign

Question 44 - Mock Exam

If your car is at least five years old and you move to New Jersey from another state, within what timeframe must you have it inspected after registering it?

- ☐   30 days
- ☐   14 days
- ☐   3 months
- ☐   6 months

Question 45 - Mock Exam

You are at a stop sign, waiting to turn right. A vehicle approaching from the left has its turn signal on. What should you do?

- ☐ Press the gas pedal immediately
- ☐ Wait until the other vehicle actually starts to turn and then start your turn
- ☐ Go ahead and turn because the other vehicle is about to turn, too
- ☐ Quickly turn on your headlights

Question 46 - Mock Exam

In New Jersey, when are you allowed to make a left turn at a red light?

- ☐ At any time
- ☐ Only when you're turning onto a one-way street
- ☐ Never
- ☐ Only when you're turning from a one-way street onto another one-way street

Question 47 - Mock Exam

What documents must you provide at the time of your road test in New Jersey?

- ☐ A valid permit
- ☐ The vehicle's registration card
- ☐ The vehicle's insurance card
- ☐ All of the above

Question 48 - Mock Exam

Under New Jersey law, which of the following groups have the same rights and responsibilities on public roadways as car and truck drivers?

- ☐ Inline skaters
- ☐ Skateboarders
- ☐ Bicyclists
- ☐ All of the above

Question 49 - Mock Exam

What should you NOT do if a tire blows out while driving?

- ☐ Ease your foot off the accelerator
- ☐ Brake immediately
- ☐ Steer straight ahead
- ☐ Grab the steering wheel firmly

Question 50 - Mock Exam

If you have already entered an intersection when the traffic light changes to yellow or red, what should you do?

- ☐ Do not proceed farther
- ☐ Stop
- ☐ Follow through and clear the intersection
- ☐ Make a left or right turn

ANSWER SHEET

PRACTICE TEST 1

Question 1 - Practice Test 1

(D) In situations where you are at least 15 years old and carry a Class A, B, C, D, or E license, you are permitted to operate a moped without needing a specific moped license.

Question 2 - Practice Test 1

(C) Overtaking another vehicle on the right side is permissible if the vehicle intends to make a left turn or if there are two or more lanes available in your direction, like on highways or one-way streets.

Question 3 - Practice Test 1

(A) Children who are under 4 years old and weigh less than 40 pounds must be secured in a federally approved rear-facing child safety seat with a five-point harness. This should be positioned in the rear seat of the vehicle. When children surpass the manufacturer's height or weight guidelines for the rear-facing seat, they should transition to a federally approved forward-facing child safety seat, also equipped with a five-point harness, located in the rear seat.

Question 4 - Practice Test 1

(C) If you're in a roundabout when an emergency vehicle with flashing lights or a siren approaches, you should continue to your designated exit, then safely pull over and let the emergency vehicle pass.

Question 5 - Practice Test 1

(D) On roads where there are two or more lanes for traffic in each direction, broken white lines serve to divide each side of the roadway into separate lanes for traffic moving in the same direction. If safe, you may cross a broken line to overtake or change lanes.

Question 6 - Practice Test 1

(D) High beam headlights should be used when there are no oncoming vehicles. They help in seeing twice as far as low beams. Use high beams on unfamiliar roads, in construction zones, or where there might be pedestrians near the road. However, low beams should be used in weather conditions like fog, rain, or snow to prevent glare caused by light reflecting back from such conditions.

Question 7 - Practice Test 1

(D) During a drive through a flooded area, you should maintain a larger distance from the vehicle ahead, be cautious with your speed considering the road conditions, and gently pump your brakes after passing through the water to dry them out and test their functionality. Applying brakes hard could lead to them locking up.

Question 8 - Practice Test 1

(A) A solid center line on your side of the road indicates that you cannot safely overtake other vehicles.

Question 9 - Practice Test 1

(A) Upon reaching the end of an on-ramp for a freeway, your speed should be as close as possible to the existing traffic's speed, depending on the ramp conditions.

Question 10 - Practice Test 1

(C) Before pulling out from a parallel parking spot on the right side of a street, you should signal a left turn and look over your left shoulder to check for incoming traffic. If you're pulling out from a parallel parking spot on the left side of a one-way street, you should signal a right turn and look over your right shoulder for incoming traffic.

Question 11 - Practice Test 1

(B) The most common locations for motorbike and automobile collisions are intersections. Usually, the automobile driver does not see the motorcycle and turns in front of it.

Question 12 - Practice Test 1

(D) The path that a vehicle's rear wheels take when turning is shorter than that of its front wheels. The difference will be more noticeable the longer the vehicle is. Before turning, tractor-trailers could at first swing out. Avoid attempting to pass a tractor-trailer on the right if you observe it moving to the left since it might be ready to make a right turn. Verify the turn signals.

Question 13 - Practice Test 1

(B) When you see a yield sign, it means that you need to slow down and get ready to stop if a car or a pedestrian is coming from the opposite direction. A car coming from the opposite direction shouldn't have to brake in order to avoid hitting you if you are approaching a yield sign.

Question 14 - Practice Test 1

(D) The left-right-left rule states that you should always look to your left when you approach an intersection because it is where the approaching traffic is closest to you. After that, turn to your right. Before continuing, take one last look to your left. On your left, you might spot a car you missed the first time you looked.

Question 15 - Practice Test 1

(C) The same-direction lanes are divided by a double solid white line, but it is not permitted to cross it. Highways frequently employ double solid white lines to demarcate high occupancy vehicle (HOV) lanes from other lanes moving in the same direction.

Question 16 - Practice Test 1

(A) Mobile devices like electronic message boards and flashing arrow panels are used on some roadways to alert drivers in advance of work zones or unusual conditions in those areas.

Question 17 - Practice Test 1

(B) You should make an effort to gaze at least one block ahead when driving in city traffic. 10 seconds is roughly one block in a metropolis.

Question 18 - Practice Test 1

(D) Avoid abruptly slowing down when leaving a two-lane, high-speed highway; you run the risk of being rear-ended by the vehicle that is in front of you. To communicate your intentions to other drivers, use your turn signals. Use the brakes to swiftly but safely slow down.

Question 19 - Practice Test 1

(C) It is crucial to keep in mind that it is irrelevant what type of alcoholic beverage is ingested. The typical beer contains the same amount of alcohol as the typical whiskey or wine. For instance, the quantity of alcohol in 1 12 ounces of 80-proof whiskey, 12 ounces of beer, or 5 ounces of wine is the same, or roughly 12 ounces per drink. According to studies, the majority of those detained for driving while intoxicated had consumed beer.

Question 20 - Practice Test 1

(C) A road intersection known as an interchange is when two or more roads cross over one another without obstructing one another's traffic. Instead, a network of linking ramps is used to connect the roads. These ramps make it possible to safely switch from one route to another without interfering with the flow of traffic. Other interchanges include folded diamond, cloverleaf, and diamond interchanges.

Question 21 - Practice Test 1

(A) You are allowed to pass a vehicle on the right in two specific scenarios: 1) when the vehicle you want to pass is preparing to make or is making a left turn, and 2) when there are at least two lanes traveling in the same direction as you, such as on a multilane highway or a one-way street. However, left-turn lanes are reserved strictly for making left turns and, where permitted, U-turns.

Question 22 - Practice Test 1

(D) As a type of regulatory sign, a "Speed Zone Ahead" sign denotes that you're approaching a zone with a reduced speed limit. Be prepared to decelerate to comply with the new speed limit.

Question 23 - Practice Test 1

(D) On a multilane road that has several lanes going in your direction, it's best to use the left-most or middle lanes for overtaking other vehicles.

Question 24 - Practice Test 1

(D) The wide white line you see painted across a lane before an intersection is known as a stop line. If there's a stop sign or red traffic light, you must stop before this line.

Question 25 - Practice Test 1

(D) The solid white line on a freeway marks its outer edge in each direction. Beyond this line is the shoulder, intended for use exclusively in emergencies. It's illegal to overtake another vehicle using the shoulder.

Question 26 - Practice Test 1

(A) If you encounter a pedestrian at an intersection using a service animal, a guide dog, or a white cane, it means they are blind or visually impaired. It's important not to honk your horn as it can startle or confuse the pedestrian or the service animal. Instead, you should stop your vehicle and yield the right-of-way.

Question 27 - Practice Test 1

(D) Applying the brakes too hard when driving at high speed can lead to a situation where the force exerted by the brakes surpasses the tires' road grip, causing the wheels to lock and the vehicle to skid irrespective of steering direction. To recover from this, release the brake pedal to unlock the wheels, then straighten the steering as the vehicle starts to regain its original path. Gradually decrease your speed until you reach a safe driving pace.

Question 28 - Practice Test 1

(A) During the process of being overtaken by another vehicle, you should avoid increasing your speed until the pass is finished.

Question 29 - Practice Test 1

(C) If your vehicle starts to submerge into water, you should try to open the window immediately. It can be difficult to open a door against the pressure of water, but windows can be rolled down with relative ease. However, power windows may malfunction due to water, so it's important to try to open them immediately.

Question 30 - Practice Test 1

(D) When there are multiple lanes traveling in the same direction, slower vehicles should ideally occupy the right-most lane, unless they are passing another vehicle or making a left turn.

Question 31 - Practice Test 1

(B) The incorrect statement here is: "At a T-intersection without control signals, vehicles on the through road should yield to those on the terminating road." In reality, at an uncontrolled T-intersection, vehicles on the terminating road should yield to those on the through road.

Question 32 - Practice Test 1

(C) If a broken yellow line appears on your side of the center dash stripe, it means you have the freedom to cross the line for overtaking other vehicles, given that it's safe to do so.

Question 33 - Practice Test 1

(D) Parking lights should be used for a short duration when your vehicle is parked, especially in zones where parking is allowed, to make your vehicle visible to other drivers. Do not use parking lights while the vehicle is in motion. If you require more illumination, you should use your headlights

Question 34 - Practice Test 1

(B) When vehicles from a different road are merging onto your roadway, you should accommodate them by adjusting your speed and the position of your vehicle, thus allowing them to merge safely.

Question 35 - Practice Test 1

(A) Being under significant physical or emotional stress can negatively affect your driving capabilities. If you're feeling exhausted, sleep-deprived, anxious, scared, angry, or depressed, you should stop driving until you feel better or let someone else take the wheel.

Question 36 - Practice Test 1

(D) The presence of various signals such as flashing lights, bells, or gates indicates that a train is either approaching or passing by. You must never disregard these signals and proceed to cross.

Question 37 - Practice Test 1

(B) You can consider it safe to merge back in front of a truck after overtaking it once you can see the entire front of the truck in your rear-view mirror.

Question 38 - Practice Test 1

(D) Every lane change requires you to perform a series of actions for safety: signaling your intentions, checking your mirrors, and looking over your shoulder to inspect your blind spots.

Question 39 - Practice Test 1

(B) If a truck is driving alongside you in the same direction, it's best to maintain as much lateral distance as possible to prevent a sideswipe incident and to minimize the wind turbulence between both vehicles.

Question 40 - Practice Test 1

(D) State law mandates that drivers adjust their speed based on current driving conditions. This includes slowing down on hills, sharp or blind curves, winding or slippery roads, or when pedestrians are nearby.

PRACTICE TEST 2

Question 1 - Practice Test 2

(B) If your vehicle gets stuck on railroad tracks and a train is coming, avoid trying to free the vehicle. Instead, ensure everyone exits the vehicle and swiftly moves at a 45-degree angle away from the tracks in the direction the train is coming. This way, you and any passengers will not be hit by debris if the car is struck. Contact 911 or call the number displayed on the railroad crossing sign.

Question 2 - Practice Test 2

(B) If you are being tailgated, change lanes if possible, or pull over to let the tailgater go by. Refrain from braking as a warning, as this could worsen an already dangerous situation. Also, do not speed up in an attempt to appease or outrun the tailgater, as some may still follow too closely.

Question 3 - Practice Test 2

(A) When double solid lines are adjacent to your lane, passing or changing lanes is prohibited.

Question 4 - Practice Test 2

(D) When driving on wet pavement at speeds up to 35 mph, modern tires generally disperse water to maintain road contact. However, at higher speeds in deep water, tire channeling becomes less effective, causing the tires to glide on the water like water skis. This phenomenon is called "hydroplaning." At 50 mph or above, hydroplaning can lead to a complete loss of braking and steering control. To avoid hydroplaning, reduce your speed.

Question 5 - Practice Test 2

(A) Warning signs are generally diamond-shaped with black letters or symbols on a yellow background.

Question 6 - Practice Test 2

(C) When the road is covered in snow, you should reduce your speed by half. On wet or icy roads, you should likewise slow down, but by a different amount.

Question 7 - Practice Test 2

(D) If confronted by an aggressive driver, do not provoke them further. Refrain from making eye contact, name-calling, or making rude gestures. For your safety, stay inside your vehicle and continue driving while slowing down and changing lanes to allow the aggressive driver to pass.

Question 8 - Practice Test 2

(D) If you experience a sudden tire blowout, firmly grip on the steering wheel and gradually release your foot off the gas pedal. Apply gentle braking only after regaining control of your vehicle.

Question 9 - Practice Test 2

(D) A solid yellow traffic light serves as a warning that the light will soon turn red. Prepare to stop for a red light, but avoid suddenly stopping if there's a vehicle close behind you to prevent a rear-end collision. If stopping safely isn't possible, cautiously proceed through the intersection.

Question 10 - Practice Test 2

(B) If your rear wheels start to skid, turn the steering wheel in the direction the vehicle is trying to go. Steer left if your rear wheels are sliding left, and steer right if they are sliding right. The rear wheels may overcorrect and begin skidding in the opposite direction; if this happens, turn the steering wheel in that direction as well. This method, known as "steering into the skid," should help regain control of your vehicle.

Question 11 - Practice Test 2

(A) If vehicles approach an intersection from opposite directions at approximately the same time, the vehicle turning left must yield to the vehicle proceeding straight or turning right.

Question 12 - Practice Test 2

(B) Four out of ten collisions are rear-end crashes, primarily caused by tailgating. Ensure at least two seconds elapse between the vehicle in front passing a stationary object and you reaching that same object. In poor or hazardous driving conditions, increase the space cushion to three or even four seconds.

Question 13 - Practice Test 2

(B) Pedestrians and vehicles already in an intersection have the right-of-way. Since a roundabout or rotary is a circular intersection, you must yield the right-of-way to pedestrians and vehicles already in the circle when entering.

Question 14 - Practice Test 2

(B) Two-thirds of deer-vehicle collisions happen in October, November, and December, which is deer breeding season. Exercise caution when driving near deer crossing signs.

Question 15 - Practice Test 2

(B) High beams allow you to see further ahead, but they can create glare by reflecting off fog, rain, or snow, making it harder to see. Use low beams in fog, rain, or snow.

Question 16 - Practice Test 2

(B) You cannot pass a vehicle on the left if your lane has a solid yellow center line. Even with a broken yellow center line, you may not pass on the left if you cannot return to the right lane before reaching a solid yellow line for that lane.

Question 17 - Practice Test 2

(A) Exit ramps allow vehicles to leave expressways. Speed limits are often reduced at exit ramps.

Question 18 - Practice Test 2

(D) If the street is too narrow for a U-turn, make a three-point turn to change your vehicle's direction. This maneuver should only be performed when the street is narrow, visibility is good, traffic is light on both sides, the turn is allowed, and no other option is available.

Question 19 - Practice Test 2

(C) A single standard alcoholic drink (1.5 ounces of liquor, 5 ounces of wine, or 12 ounces of beer) can raise your blood alcohol content (BAC) to 0.02% or higher. At a BAC of 0.02%, your ability to track a moving target visually and perform two tasks simultaneously is impaired.

Question 20 - Practice Test 2

(D) When another vehicle is passing you on the left, reduce your speed slightly and maintain your position in the center of your lane until the vehicle has safely passed and is ahead of you. Once the vehicle has safely passed, you can resume your normal speed.

Question 21 - Practice Test 2

(D) When turning right on a multi-lane road, you should generally use the rightmost lane, unless signs, signals, or lane markings permit turning from multiple lanes.

Question 22 - Practice Test 2

(B) When an emergency vehicle with flashing lights, a siren, or an air horn is approaching you from any direction, you should pull over to the right and stop. However, if you are already in an intersection, proceed through the intersection before stopping.

Question 23 - Practice Test 2

(C) Flashing red lights, lowered crossing gates, or ringing bells at a railroad crossing indicate that a train is approaching or passing. You must stop at least 15 feet from the nearest rail of the tracks and remain stopped until the lights or bells have stopped and the crossing gates are fully raised.

Question 24 - Practice Test 2

(C) You should not pass a vehicle on the right if it is making or about to make a right turn. Ensure the passing lane is clear before attempting to pass.

Question 25 - Practice Test 2

(A) When driving in open country at night, use your high-beam headlights, as they allow you to see much further than low beams.

Question 26 - Practice Test 2

(B) Crosswalks can be either marked or unmarked, and they may be present whether or not there are crosswalk lines.

Question 27 - Practice Test 2

(D) Tractor-trailers often appear to be moving slower than they actually are due to their large size. Maintain a safe distance and be cautious when passing around them.

Question 28 - Practice Test 2

(D) Always look both ways at railroad crossings, crosswalks, and intersections. Be sure to follow the left-right-left rule to check for approaching pedestrians, vehicles, or trains.

Question 29 - Practice Test 2

(A) You should always signal before passing another vehicle to ensure safe and clear communication with other drivers on the road.

Question 30 - Practice Test 2

(A) Your horn should be used to warn pedestrians or other drivers of potential danger. However, avoid using your horn unnecessarily or to express anger at others, as this can be a sign of aggressive driving.

Question 31 - Practice Test 2

(D) The type of alcohol does not affect your BAC, as the amount of ethanol matters rather than the form it takes. All alcoholic drinks contain different amounts of ethanol, but 1.5 ounces of 80-proof liquor, 5 ounces of wine, 12 ounces of beer, and 12 ounces of wine cooler have the same amount of ethanol.

Question 32 - Practice Test 2

(C) As the driver, you are responsible for ensuring all children in the vehicle are properly secured. Fines and penalty points may apply for each violation.

Question 33 - Practice Test 2

(C) The appropriate hand signal for a right turn is a left arm bent at 90 degrees, pointing upward.

Question 34 - Practice Test 2

(C) Treat a flashing red light like a stop sign, meaning you must stop before entering the intersection, yield to traffic and pedestrians, and proceed when safe.

Question 35 - Practice Test 2

(A) Bridges, overpasses, and ramps are especially vulnerable to icing because they are exposed to more moisture and cold air. When driving on these surfaces in freezing weather, use caution.

Question 36 - Practice Test 2

(C) Vehicles already on the expressway have the right-of-way when a vehicle is merging.

Question 37 - Practice Test 2

(D) Stopping in the middle of an intersection is illegal, even for approaching emergency vehicles. Instead, continue through the intersection and pull over immediately afterward.

Question 38 - Practice Test 2

(C) At an all-way stop, yield to vehicles that arrived before you. Vehicles should proceed in the order they arrived, with the first vehicle to arrive going first.

Question 39 - Practice Test 2

(C) Blind pedestrians have the absolute right-of-way. Yield to the pedestrian, stopping if necessary. Avoid honking your horn near a blind pedestrian, as it may startle them or mask essential auditory cues.

Question 40 - Practice Test 2

(B) It is likely safe to merge back in front of the vehicle once you can see its entire front bumper in your rear-view mirror.

ROAD SIGNS

Question 1 - Road Signs

(A) The image illustrates that overtaking on the left is permissible when the road ahead is clear. Overtaking and passing should be done with caution due to oncoming traffic.

Question 2 - Road Signs

(D) This sign denotes that a rest area is available on the right.

Question 3 - Road Signs

(C) This warning sign indicates the presence of a playground ahead.

Question 4 - Road Signs

(A) This sign warns drivers that a nearby side road crosses a railroad track. When turning onto the side road, proceed with caution.

Question 5 - Road Signs

(C) This sign denotes that you are not permitted to park in a handicap zone unless you have the necessary permit.

Question 6 - Road Signs

(C) A vehicle with a reflective triangular orange sign on the rear identifies it as a low-speed or slow-moving vehicle, which is typically defined as a motor vehicle with a top speed of no more than 25 mph. Farm vehicles and road maintenance vehicles are examples of these type of slow-moving vehicles. Slow down and proceed with caution if you come across one of these vehicles.

Question 7 - Road Signs

(B) The blue-and-white signs direct you to services such as gas stations, fast food restaurants, motels, and hospitals. Picture B indicates that there is a hospital ahead.

Question 8 - Road Signs

(C) In this case the larger sign alerts you to the impending arrival of a speed zone. The speed limit is indicated by the smaller sign. The speed limit will be reduced to 45 mph ahead in this case. So be prepared to slow down so that you don't go over the speed limit.

Question 9 - Road Signs

(A) Typically, vertical rectangular signs provide instructions or inform you of traffic laws. Drivers, pedestrians, and cyclists are given instructions by such regulatory signs.

Question 10 - Road Signs

(C) This sign denotes that the road ahead curves in the direction indicated by the arrow.

Question 11 - Road Signals Full

(A) This is a warning sign that may be placed ahead of the railroad crossing. Vehicles must slow down, look, listen, and be prepared to stop at the crossing ahead.

Question 12 - Road Signs

(A) The sequential arrow panels can be used in work zones 24 hours a day, seven days a week. This sign indicates that the lane ahead is closed and that you should take the lane to your left.

Question 13 - Road Signs

(C) This sign denotes that the divided highway is ending ahead. The road will be converted to a two-way street. Keep to the right and keep an eye out for oncoming traffic.

Question 14 - Road Signs

(B) This sign is normally displayed at an intersection with a combination of signals, including a green arrow pointing left. When the green arrow is lit, you may make a protected left turn; oncoming traffic will be stopped at a red light. This sign indicates that if the green arrow disappears and a steady green light appears, you may still make a left turn, but you must now yield to oncoming traffic before turning.

Question 15 - Road Signs

(B) A disabled crossing is indicated by the sign ahead. Slow down and take your time.

Question 16 - Road Signs

(D) This indicates a warning signal. Bicyclists and pedestrians frequently cross the road in the vicinity of the sign. You must drive cautiously and be prepared to stop.

Question 17 - Road Signs

(B) This sign denotes a bicycle crossing. This sign forewarns you that a bikeway will cross the road ahead.

Question 18 - Road Signs

(C) If you see this sign while driving in the left lane, you should turn left at the next intersection.

Question 19 - Road Signs

(D) This warning sign indicates that there will be a double curve ahead. The road ahead bends to the right, then to the left. (A winding road sign would be posted instead if there was a triple curve ahead.) Slow down, stay to the right, and do not pass.

Question 20 - Road Signs

(D) The pedestrian signals are only used to direct pedestrian traffic. This pedestrian signal indicates that pedestrians may enter the crosswalk to cross the road. (Older signals displayed the word "WALK" instead.) A signal with an upraised hand warns pedestrians not to enter the crosswalk. (Older signals displayed the words "DO NOT WALK" instead.)

Question 21 - Road Signs

(A) This navigational sign indicates the presence of a hospital ahead.

Question 22 - Road Signs

(A) This symbol indicates an exit number. This is the number assigned to a highway exit at a junction. If an interchange has more than one exit, a letter may be added to indicate which exit it is: For example: 117A, 117B, and so on.

Question 23 - Road Signs

(A) This is a gas station service sign

Question 24 - Road Signs

(C) This is a speed advisory sign at a roundabout. In the roundabout, the speed limit is 15 mph.

Question 25 - Road Signs

(A) This is a traffic control sign. This sign indicates that traffic must only make a left turn.

Question 26 - Road Signs

(A) The arrow signifies a right turn. In contrast, a red slash inside a red circle symbolizes "no." Turning right is prohibited by this regulatory sign. This sign is typically located on the right side of the road or above a driving lane.

Question 27 - Road Signs

(B) This service sign indicates that a telephone service is available ahead.

Question 28 - Road Signs

(B) This sign is next to a route marker sign. It indicates that you will need to turn right soon to enter or continue on that route.

Question 29 - Road Signs

(B) This sign shows the safest speed to enter or depart an expressway. Reduce your speed to the specified speed (in this case, 30 mph).

Question 30 - Road Signs

(B) A single broken (dashed) yellow line may exist on a two-lane, two-way road. Vehicles on either side may pass if it is safe to do so.

Question 31 - Road Signs

(D) Lane use control signs are rectangular, black-and-white signs that indicate whether or not turning from specific lanes is required at an intersection. You are only permitted to drive in the direction indicated for your traffic lane.

Question 32 - Road Signs

(B) This sign shows the presence of a four-way intersection ahead. Drivers should be alert for cross traffic entering the roadway.

Question 33 - Road Signs

(A) This sign indicates a low-ground clearance railroad crossing. The railroad crossing is elevated enough that a vehicle with a large wheelbase or limited ground clearance could become stranded on the tracks. A car driver should have no trouble navigating this type of railroad crossing unless he or she is towing a trailer or driving a mobile home with low ground clearance.

Question 34 - Road Signs

(B) If your lane has a broken or dashed line (white or yellow), you may pass if it is safe to do so.

Question 35 - Road Signs

(C) A stop sign is an eight-sided white-on-red sign that indicates other traffic has the right-of-way. Always come to a complete stop before proceeding and yield to approaching vehicles.

Question 36 - Road Signs

(D) Work zone signs notify drivers of unusual or potentially hazardous conditions on or around the traveled route. These signs include black lettering or symbols on an orange background. If you encounter these signals, slow down and pay close attention.

Question 37 - Road Signs

(A) The shape of the arrow indicates that you are going to enter a winding road. A winding road has at least three turns. Take your time and slow down.

Question 38 - Road Signs

(C) When the road surface is wet, it becomes slippery. This sign is frequently found near bridges and overpasses.

Question 39 - Road Signs

(B) This is a freeway interchange sign. This sign warns you that you are approaching an interchange.

Question 40 - Road Signs

(D) This sign indicates that you must never park on the left side of the sign.

Question 41 - Road Signs

(B) This sign advises that the road ahead will be divided into two lanes. To separate opposing lanes, a divider, also known as a median, will be used. Continue right.

Question 42 - Road Signs

(B) This sign indicates that you are driving in the wrong way. Turn around.

Question 43 - Road Signs

(D) This sign denotes that the maximum nighttime speed limit is 45 mph.

Question 44 - Road Signs

(A) This is an emergency vehicle warning sign. It indicates the possibility of emergency vehicles from fire stations or other emergency facilities entering the route. If an emergency vehicle approaches from any direction and is sounding a siren, blowing an air horn, or flashing lights, you must surrender to it.

Question 45 - Road Signs

(D) This sign can be located at the end of various T-intersections. It means that before turning right or left onto the through route, you must yield the right of way or come to a complete stop.

Question 46 - Road Signs

(C) This sign indicates that U-turns are not permitted in this area.

Question 47 - Road Signs

(B) This sign indicates a T-junction. This sign indicates that the road you're on is about to come to an end. Prepare to make a right or left turn. Yield to oncoming traffic.

Question 48 - Road Signs

(A) This is an animal crossing sign. In this area, the animal represented on the sign (in this case, a deer) is common. Keep a watch out for animals like this crossing the street, particularly at dawn and night. Deer, elk, and other species roam in herds. Keep an eye out for more if you spot one. A collision with a large animal has the potential to kill the animal, do significant damage to your vehicle.

Question 49 - Road Signs

(C) This sign warns drivers not to exceed the specified speed limit in a school zone or school crossing when there are children present. In this scenario, the maximum permissible speed is 15 mph.

Question 50 - Road Signs

(B) This sign is indicating a service. It is recommended that drivers use lodging facilities if necessary.

Question 51 - Road Signs

(A) This white diamond sign shows that the road is reserved for high-occupancy vehicles (HOVs) at the times specified from Monday to Friday.

Question 52 - Road Signs

(D) At an intersection, a stop sign accompanied by this sign denotes that the intersection is a four-way stop. Each approaching road has a stop sign and a "4-Way" sign.

Question 53 - Road Signs

(B) This sign warns you that you are approaching a T-intersection from the terminating roadway. At the T-intersection, you must turn left or right after yielding the right-of-way to through traffic if necessary.

Question 54 - Road Signs

(A) This sign advises you to turn right onto Route 47 and go north.

Question 55 - Road Signs

(B) This is a guide sign indicating that you are approaching an airport.

Question 56 - Road Signs

(A) This sign denotes the presence of a side road ahead. Keep an eye out for oncoming vehicles from that direction.

Question 57 - Road Signs

(B) This sign indicates a sharp left turn. Slow down (in this case, to the recommended speed of 25 mph), keep right as you turn, and do not pass

Question 58 - Road Signs

(D) A speed limit sign specifies the top legal speed allowed on the expressway under ideal driving circumstances.

Question 59 - Road Signs

C) This sign warns of a road closure ahead, yet an alternate route is only 1,000 feet away.

Question 60 - Road Signs

(B) This sign indicates that there will be a bump in the road ahead. To avoid losing control, slow down.

Question 61 - Road Signs

(B) White lines separate traffic lanes traveling in the same direction. You must drive between the lane markings.

Question 62 - Road Signs

(C) This sign indicates that road maintenance is being done. Slow down, exercise caution, and follow all signs and instructions. Move into a lane that is further away from the workers if feasible.

Question 63 - Road Signs

(A) Most warning signs are diamond-shaped with a yellow background. This sign warns you that a stop sign is about to appear. Prepare to come to a complete stop and yield. Before any stop line or crosswalk placed on the pavement, you must come to a complete stop.

Question 64 - Road Signs

(C) This pentagonal (five-sided) sign indicates that you are approaching a school zone and be cautious.

Question 65 - Road Signs

(D) A prohibitory sign with a red circle and slash symbolizes "no." This sign advises that no left turns are allowed in this location.

Question 66 - Road Signs

(B) This sign denotes an exit number. These signs point you in the direction of bike routes, parking lots, mile markers, and specific exits. Enter the milepost number and the exit number to see how far you are from the exit you want to take.

Question 67 - Road Signs

This symbol represents a soft shoulder. The dirt along the road is soft. Never, unless in an emergency, leave the pavement.

Question 68 - Road Signs

(A) This sign indicates that a traffic island or divider is ahead. Maintain your position to the left of this stumbling block.

Question 69 - Road Signs

(A) A red slash inside a red circle means "no." This sign indicates that driving on railroad tracks are prohibited.

Question 70 - Road Signs

(D) A red slash inside a red circle means "no." According to this regulatory sign, pedestrians are not permitted to cross here.

Question 71 - Road Signs

(A) Lanes of traffic moving in the opposing directions are divided by yellow lines. A solid yellow line should only be crossed while turning left.

Question 72 - Road Signs

(D) The presence of a flagger (flag person) is indicated by this work zone sign. Construction zones on highways or streets typically have flaggers present. To safely direct traffic through certain places, they wear orange vests, shirts, or jackets and wave red flags or use STOP/SLOW paddles. Follow the flagger's instructions.

Question 73 - Road Signs

(A) When you see this sign while driving on the main road, be prepared for other cars and trucks to enter your lane.

Question 74 - Road Signs

(A) This is a warning sign noting that a narrow bridge is ahead. Although the bridge has two lanes of traffic, there is very little clearance.

Question 75 - Road Signs

(B) This sort of warning sign notifies drivers in advance of a lane reduction. This sign signals that the right lane is about to stop. Drivers in the right lane must merge to the left. Drivers in the left lane should allow vehicles in the right lane to merge smoothly.

Question 76 - Road Signs

(A) This sign indicates a bicycle lane intended for bicyclists. Normally, cars and trucks should not use this lane. In many (but not all) states, cars, and trucks may travel in this lane for a short distance when ready to turn at the next intersection.

Question 77 - Road Signs

(A) A Y-intersection is represented by this symbol. The road ahead is divided into two halves. If traffic crosses your path, be prepared to turn in either direction.

Question 78 - Road Signs

(D) Guide signs provide information to drivers regarding the sort of route they are on, forthcoming highway entrances and exits, and distances to various destinations. Guide signs in the shape of a shield are often used to indicate US Routes and interstate highways. This sign indicates that you are on Interstate 95 (I-95), which connects Maine and Florida.

Question 79 - Road Signs

(C) The sign features the International Symbol of Access for Disabled People. This means that only those with disability parking permits will be able to use these spaces. To park in these areas, you must get a disability parking placard or disabled license plates from your state.

Question 80 - Road Signs

(B) This sign alerts drivers to the presence of cattle on the route.

Question 81 - Road Signs

(C) In North America, raising one's hand with the thumb expresses a desire to hitch a ride. A red slash inside a red circle means "no." Hitchhiking is illegal on this stretch of road, according to this sign. Please do not stop here to pick up hitchhikers.

Question 82 - Road Signs

(D) This is a route marker sign for the United States. A route marker sign's shape and color identify the type of road you're on. Shield-shaped signs are commonly used to indicate US Routes and interstate routes. This sign shows that you are on US Highway 40. The United States Routes are a network of roads and highways that were built decades before the Interstate Highway System. US Route 40 was built in 1926 and goes from Silver Summit, Utah to Atlantic City, New Jersey.

Question 83 - Road Signs

(C) This symbol indicates that a pedestrian crosswalk is ahead. Drivers must give pedestrians the right of way.

Question 84 - Road Signs

(A) This is a wayfinding sign. This indicates that food is available

Question 85 - Road Signs

(C) If you notice this sign and are traveling slower than the majority of traffic, change to the right lane so that quicker traffic on the left can pass you.

Question 86 - Road Signs

(B) This one-way sign instructs drivers to only proceed in the direction indicated by the arrow.

Question 87 - Road Signs

(D) According to this sign, the main road will bend to the left, with a side road entering from the right. When approaching this crossroads, use additional caution. A car arriving from around the curve who is ready to enter the main road from a side road may not spot you approaching from around the curve and may pull out in front of you.

Question 88 - Road Signs

(D) This sign indicates that traffic may flow on both sides of the road.

Question 89 - Road Signs

(C) The speed restriction is 40 miles per hour, as shown by this sign. In ideal conditions, this is the fastest you can travel.

Question 90 - Road Signs

(C) This sign cautions that a low point on the road is ahead. Slow down for your own peace of mind and control. Proceed with caution and be ready to turn around if the dip becomes flooded.

Question 91 - Road Signs

(B) This sign indicates alternate routes during road closures or construction. Take note of these cues.

Question 92 - Road Signs

(D) A white line separates two lanes traveling in the same direction. To pass or change lanes, you may cross a broken line. If it's a straight line, you should normally stay in your lane.

Question 93 - Road Signs

(D) This sign regulates traffic and instructs drivers whether to turn left or straight.

Question 94 - Road Signs

(C) A red slash inside a red circle means "no." The wording on this regulatory sign is "No Parking." Parking is not allowed at this sign.

Question 95 - Road Signs

(B) This sign instructs you to proceed straight. You can't turn around here.

Question 96 - Road Signs

(C) The center lane is for left turns (or U-turns when allowed) and can be utilized by vehicles traveling in either direction. On the pavement, left-turn arrows for one-way traffic alternate with left-turn arrows for the opposite direction. These lanes are denoted by solid and broken (dashed) yellow lines on each side.

Question 97 - Road Signs

(B) A yield sign is the only form of sign with a downward-pointing triangle shape. Before proceeding, you must slow down and yield to oncoming traffic and pedestrians when you come to a yield sign. Be prepared to make a stop for them as well.

Question 98 - Road Signs

(B) This unusual lane control sign informs that all vehicles in this lane must make a U-turn. This sign may be accompanied by a traffic signal, with illuminated U-turn arrows showing when vehicles can do U-turns.

Question 99 - Road Signs

(B) Mileposts are spaced at regular intervals to keep drivers aware of them. They are placed along the road's edge to convey information to drivers about their location on the roadway for navigation and emergency purposes. The number on the milepost usually indicates the distance in miles to the state line or the end of the road.

Question 100 - Road Signs

(B) The majority of public crossings have crossbuck signs and railroad flashing light signals. The same rules that apply to YIELD signs apply to these signs as well.

SIGNS AND SITUATIONS

Question 1 - Signs and Situations

(D) Lane use control signals are special overhead signals that indicate which lanes of a roadway may be utilized in various directions at different times. A flashing yellow "X" denotes that this lane is solely for left turns.

Question 2 - Signs and Situations

(D) Vehicles moving in either direction must stop at least 20 feet from a school bus that has stopped with its red lights flashing. They must remain stopped until the bus starts its motion or until the bus driver or a traffic police waves them on.

Question 3 - Signs and Situations

(D) This is a reserved lane. This lane is restricted to specific types of vehicles. High-occupancy vehicle (HOV) lanes and bus lanes are two examples. Keep an eye out for signs stating which cars are permitted to use the lane.

Question 4 - Signs and Situations

(C) When two vehicles approach an intersection at roughly the same moment, the vehicle on the left must yield to the one on the right. In the absence of this rule, the vehicle turning left must yield to approaching traffic. Car A must yield to Car B in this situation.

Question 5 - Signs and Situations

(A) If your brakes fail while driving downhill, the vehicle may begin to roll forward. You can configure the transmission to counteract this movement. Set your manual transmission to Reverse. Set the automatic transmission to Park if you have one.

Question 6 - Signs and Situations

(C) At an uncontrolled intersection, a vehicle must yield to pedestrians in a marked or unmarked crosswalk. After considering pedestrians, each vehicle must yield to the one on its right. Consequently, Vehicle C must yield to Vehicle B, and Vehicle A must yield to Vehicle C.

Question 7 - Signs and Situations

(B) When passing a stopped emergency vehicle, you must slow down. If possible, also change to a non-adjacent lane, leaving at least one empty lane between you and the emergency vehicle.

Question 8 - Signs and Situations

(C) If your vehicle's brakes fail while parked uphill, it may start rolling backward. To counter this movement, set your transmission accordingly. For manual transmissions, set it to first gear for maximum forward torque. For automatic transmissions, set it to Park.

Question 9 - Signs and Situations

(B) Always follow directions from a police officer, even if it means disregarding other traffic devices or rules. For example, drive through a red light or stop sign if a police officer waves you through.

Question 10 - Signs and Situations

(B) Consider a flashing red signal to be a STOP sign. That is, you must come to a complete stop before crossing the intersection, yield to oncoming vehicles and pedestrians, and then proceed cautiously when it is safe to do so.

Question 11 - Signs and Situations

(A) When railroad crossing signals indicate an approaching train, stop at least 15 feet from the nearest rail. Trains are at least six feet wider than the tracks they run on, so maintain a safe distance. Even after the train passes, signals may continue to flash or sound and the gate may stay lowered, indicating a second train is approaching.

Question 12 - Signs and Situations

(A) You must come to a complete stop and yield to all traffic and pedestrians ahead. You can then proceed when the intersection is clear and there are no vehicles approaching that may present a hazard.

Question 13 - Signs and Situations

(A) High-occupancy vehicle (HOV) lanes are designed for vehicles with multiple occupants. This sign means that this lane is an HOV 2+ lane, which requires at least two occupants in each vehicle. In other words, a driver and at least one passenger. An HOV 3+ lane would require a driver and at least two passengers.

Question 14 - Signs and Situations

(A) When two vehicles arrive at an uncontrolled intersection about the same time, the vehicle on the left must yield. Car A must yield in this situation.

Question 15 - Signs and Situations

(C) After yielding to all pedestrians and vehicles already in the junction, you can proceed on a green signal.

Question 16 - Signs and Situations

(A) If you have a green light, you may continue through the intersection, but you must first yield to all pedestrians and vehicles already in the intersection. In this case, Car A must yield to Car B since Car B has already entered the intersection.

Question 17 - Signs and Situations

(C) Prior to making a left turn off the road, you must yield to all pedestrians and oncoming traffic.

Question 18 - Signs and Situations

(B) When a school bus driver activates the flashing yellow lights just before stopping for passengers, you should slow down and prepare to stop. Once the school bus's red lights start flashing, you must stop at least 20 feet away from the bus.

Question 19 - Signs and Situations

(D) At a STOP sign, you must stop before the stop line. If there isn't a stop line, stop before the crosswalk. If there isn't a crosswalk either, stop before entering the intersection.

Question 20 - Signs and Situations

(B) You may turn left on a green light after yielding to pedestrians, oncoming vehicles, and vehicles already in the intersection.

Question 21 - Signs and Situations

(A) When parking uphill parallel to a curb, point your wheels away from the curb and allow your vehicle to roll back slightly so the rear part of the front wheel on the curb side rests against the curb. If your brakes fail, the curb will prevent your car from rolling backward. Ensure you still engage your parking brake and leave your car in the appropriate gear.

Question 22 - Signs and Situations

(B) Upon encountering a stopped emergency vehicle, sanitation vehicle, utility vehicle, or tow truck with flashing lights, move to a non-adjacent lane if possible, leaving at least one vacant lane between your vehicle and the stopped vehicle. If this isn't possible or is unsafe, slow down as you pass the vehicle.

Question 23 - Signs and Situations

(A) The driver intends to turn left.

Question 24 - Signs and Situations

(A) When an emergency vehicle approaches you from either direction with its siren and flashing lights activated, you must clear any intersection, yield to the emergency vehicle, pull over to the nearest edge of the road, and remain stopped until the emergency vehicle has passed.

Question 25 - Signs and Situations

(D) You must signal for at least 100 feet before making a turn. Even if no other vehicles are visible, you must still signal. The most dangerous vehicle could be the one you don't see.

FINE & LIMITS

Question 1 - Fines & Limits

(A) If it's your first violation, you'll be penalized $100 to $500 and your license might be suspended for up to two years if you abandon the vehicle on a limited-access highway for four hours or more. Penalties for a second or subsequent infraction include a $500–$1,000 fine and a five–year license suspension.

Question 2 - Fines & Limits

(D) You will be compelled to pay all of the following if you are found guilty of your first DUI offense: a fine between $250 and $500, a surcharge of $1,000 annually for three years, a daily fee to the IDRC (Intoxicated Driver Resource Center), a fee of $100 to the drunk driving fund, a fee of $75 to Safe Neighborhood Services, and a fee of $100 to the AERF (Alcohol Education and Rehabilitation Fund).

Question 3 - Fines & Limits

(B) If you are found guilty of drinking and driving twice, you will have to perform 10 days of community service and pay a $250 fine.

Question 4 - Fines & Limits

(C) You will receive two points on your driving record if you are found guilty of passing past a safety zone. A Safety Zone is a clearly designated area designated for pedestrian usage (for instance, the area where people board or disembark buses).

Question 5 - Fines & Limits

(D) Two points will be added to your driving record if you are found guilty of operating a vehicle on a sidewalk.

Question 6 - Fines & Limits

(B) Alcohol is broken down by your body at a regular rate. The average time it takes for the alcohol in one "standard" drink you've had to break down is one hour. 1.5 ounces of hard liquor, 5 ounces of wine, or 12 ounces of beer constitute one normal drink. This rate cannot be raised by coffee, exercise, or a cold shower. You must wait until all of the alcohol in your system has been eliminated by your body.

Question 7 - Fines & Limits

(A) If you are found guilty of your first DUI conviction, you might receive a sentence of up to 30 days in jail.

Question 8 - Fines & Limits

(A) If it was your first violation, your license will be suspended for a year if you are found guilty of operating a vehicle without liability insurance. However, if you can show the court that you have liability insurance presently, this suspension time can be shortened or perhaps erased.

Question 9 - Fines & Limits

(C) When your license is restored after a first-time DUI conviction, you must install an ignition interlock device (IID) in every car you drive for a minimum of three months. If your blood alcohol content (BAC) was between 0.08% and 0.10% at the time of the violation, the minimum IID installation duration is three months. Your BAC will be monitored by the IID, and if it rises beyond a defined threshold, it will prevent your car from starting.

Question 10 - Fines & Limits

(D) If you are found guilty of reckless driving for the first time, you might spend up to 60 days in jail and/or be required to pay a fine between $50 and $200. A fine of $100 to $500 or both may be imposed, together with a sentence of up to three months in jail, for a second offense.

DISTRACTED DRIVING

Question 1 - Distracted Driving

(B) It is preferable to use a hands-free or speaker phone while driving if you are an adult driver and absolutely must use your phone. In several states, it is illegal and not advised to use a mobile phone while driving.

Question 2 - Distracted Driving

(C) Never turn around to attend to the needs of passengers, kids, or animals while you are driving. Pull over to the side of the road and park your vehicle if you need to attend to any passengers or animals.

Question 3 - Distracted Driving

(A) Although stimulants, physical activity, and music can help you stay alert, sleeping is the greatest cure for fatigue. Consult a doctor if, despite receiving 9 hours of sleep, you still feel exhausted.

Question 4 - Distracted Driving

(D) Before taking a medication, look for any warnings about its effect(s) while you are driving. Ask your doctor or pharmacist about any potential side effects if you are unsure if it is safe to take the medication and drive. Drugs used to treat headaches, colds, hay fever or other allergies, or to calm nerves might cause drowsiness and have an impact on a person's ability to drive. Similar to how alcohol does, some prescription medications can impair your reflexes, judgment, eyesight, and awareness.

Question 5 - Distracted Driving

(C) Many over-the-counter and prescription drugs might make you sleepy. Only use drugs while driving if your doctor says they won't impair your ability to drive safely.

Question 6 - Distracted Driving

(D) Texting while driving currently accounts for 25% of all car accidents in the US and is the greatest cause of death for youths. Texting while driving is illegal.

Question 7 - Distracted Driving

(A) Talking on a cell phone while driving increases your chances of being in a crash by up to four times. This is because the talk is taking your focus away from driving. Sending text messages (texting) while driving increases your chances of being in an accident by up to eightfold.

Question 8 - Distracted Driving

(D) Cell phones are not permitted to be used by underage drivers while driving, unless to notify an emergency.

Question 9 - Distracted Driving

(D) Distractions, even on straight roads or empty roads, should be avoided. Refrain from eating, drinking, smoking, texting, reading, or engaging in difficult conversations while driving. If possible, turn off your phone and keep it off until you have completed driving for the day.

Question 10 - Distracted Driving

(D) Fatigue can impair your judgement, slow down your reaction times, and decrease your awareness of your surroundings.

Question 11 - Distracted Driving

(D) Distractions while driving include text messaging, talking on the phone, dealing with children, and lighting a cigarette, among other activities that draw your attention away from the road.

Question 12 - Distracted Driving

(D) Over-the-counter drugs, prescription drugs, and illegal drugs can all impact your ability to drive safely.

Question 13 - Distracted Driving

(B) Highway hypnosis or drowsiness while driving can result from monotonous road and traffic conditions, the hum of wind, tires, and the engine. Drivers can avoid highway hypnosis by continuously moving their eyes and monitoring traffic and road signs around them.

Question 14 - Distracted Driving

(D) Activities that require the use of your hands should be avoided while driving. Listening to the radio, however, can help you stay alert.

Question 15 - Distracted Driving

(B) It is against the law for minors to use a cell phone while driving. If a cell phone rings, they should not answer the call. Violators of this law may face fines.

Question 16 - Distracted Driving

(C) You should set up your cab before starting your trip but eating and drinking should be done at rest stops.

Question 17 - Distracted Driving

(A) Driving while operating a visual screen device or texting is illegal and prohibited by law.

Question 18 - Distracted Driving

(D) You should also be aware of potential distractions and impairments, as they can affect your driving abilities. All the listed factors, including emotional and physical states like fatigue, anger, illness, stress, and fear, can impair your driving skills.

Question 19 - Distracted Driving

(D) Texting or eating while driving increases the risk of an accident. If you are lost, pull over and input navigation instructions. However, using audio navigation while driving is permitted.

Question 20 - Distracted Driving

(D) It is risky to do anything while driving that diverts your attention from the road, including getting dressed, putting on makeup, reading, eating, or drinking. Take care not to hold someone in your lap, or a pet or parcel in your arms.

DRINKING AND DRIVING

Question 1 - Drinking and Driving

(D) Refusing to undergo mandatory blood and/or urine tests may result in the suspension of your driving privilege.

Question 2 - Drinking and Driving

(A) Only time can effectively eliminate alcohol from a person's system. Coffee and fresh air might alleviate some symptoms of intoxication but will not reduce the actual level of impairment.

Question 3 - Drinking and Driving

(D) Upon conviction of driving under the influence of alcohol or drugs, penalties may include license suspension, significant fines, and community service.

Question 4 - Drinking and Driving

(A) Alcohol consumption impairs vision, slows reactions, and affects judgment but does not increase alertness.

Question 5 - Drinking and Driving

(D) A standard serving of alcohol is typically 1.5 ounces, regardless of the type of drink.

Question 6 - Drinking and Driving

(C) Drinking alcohol and driving at night is especially risky because vision is already restricted due to darkness.

Question 7 - Drinking and Driving

(D) The type of alcohol does not affect blood alcohol concentration, as standard servings of different types of alcohol contain the same amount of alcohol.

Question 8 - Drinking and Driving

(D) Even small amounts of alcohol can impair a driver's reflexes, driving skills, and depth perception.

Question 9 - Drinking and Driving

(D) License suspension is mandatory for minors convicted of driving under the influence of drugs or transporting an open container of any alcoholic beverage.

Question 10 - Drinking and Driving

(B) Drunk driving is the leading cause of death among young Americans aged 16 to 24, with alcohol-related crashes occurring every 33 minutes.

Question 11 - Drinking and Driving

(D) Open containers of alcohol are only allowed in areas inaccessible to drivers or passengers, such as trunks, cargo areas, or truck beds.

Question 12 - Drinking and Driving

(D) Alcohol can impact your concentration, reaction time, and judgment.

Question 13 - Drinking and Driving

(D) Consuming alcohol before or while driving can diminish a driver's reflexes, physical control of the vehicle, and awareness of potential dangers on the road.

Question 14 - Drinking and Driving

(A) Drivers under 21 are not permitted to buy, consume, or possess alcohol.

Question 15 - Drinking and Driving

(A) The liver can process approximately one standard drink per hour. If you consume a large amount of alcohol, it may take a day or two for your body to fully recover.

Question 16 - Drinking and Driving

(A) Open container laws prohibit open containers of alcohol in areas accessible to the driver or passengers of a vehicle, with exceptions for limousines, taxis, motor homes, and commercial buses.

Question 17 - Drinking and Driving

(D) If you plan to drink alcohol, consider using public transportation, a taxi, or designating a sober driver to get home safely.

Question 18 - Drinking and Driving

(D) Drivers under the influence of alcohol are more likely to drive too fast or too slow, change lanes frequently, and fail to dim headlights.

Question 19 - Drinking and Driving

(D) For minors between the ages of 15 and 21, it is illegal to possess, consume, attempt to purchase, or purchase alcohol, or have a BAC of 0.02% or higher.

Question 20 - Drinking and Driving

(D) Alcohol enters the bloodstream and affects various bodily processes, such as coordination, self-control, and reaction time. The only way to counteract alcohol's impact on the brain is to wait for it to leave the bloodstream.

EXAM TEST PRACTICE

.

Question 1 - Mock Exam

(A) On divided highways and one-way roads, solid yellow lines serve as lines indicating the left edge.

Question 2 - Mock Exam

(B) In construction zones, speed limits are usually decreased. Remember, in New Jersey, speeding fines double in these areas.

Question 3 - Mock Exam

(C) New Jersey regulations forbid parking within 10 feet of a fire hydrant. Make sure to also observe other signage that might restrict or limit parking.

Question 4 - Mock Exam

(B) The longer the vehicle, the larger the discrepancy between the paths of the front and rear wheels when turning. Consequently, buses and tractor-trailers may initially move left before making a right turn. If you see a bus or a tractor-trailer drifting left, do not attempt to pass it on the right. It may be preparing to make a right turn. Check its turn signals.

Question 5 - Mock Exam

(D) Various substances, including alcohol, certain illegal drugs, some prescription medicines, and some over-the-counter medications, can cause sedation, drowsiness, or impaired coordination, thus affecting driving abilities. Pep pills and other stimulants can make you anxious, dizzy, or unable to concentrate, and they can also affect your vision. If you are unsure about the side effects of a particular medicine, check the warning label or consult your pharmacist or doctor.

Question 6 - Mock Exam

(B) When two or more lanes are moving in the same direction, slower vehicles should use the right lane, except when passing or preparing to turn left.

Question 7 - Mock Exam

(A) Hard braking on a slippery road might lock the wheels and cause skidding. However, if your vehicle is equipped with anti-lock brakes (ABS), they will automatically adjust if a wheel starts to lock. If your vehicle does not have ABS, pumping the brakes can help prevent wheel lock.

Question 8 - Mock Exam

(C) When the driver's left arm is extended downward out the window, it's an indication that they intend to slow down or stop.

Question 9 - Mock Exam

(C) Under normal circumstances, you should stop for a stopped school bus with flashing red lights, regardless of the direction it is facing. However, in New Jersey, there is an exception: if the school bus is on the other side of a divided highway, you are allowed to proceed but your speed should not exceed 10 mph.

Question 10 - Mock Exam

(D) Unless otherwise indicated, the maximum speed limit on rural roads is 50 mph.

Question 11 - Mock Exam

(D) In New Jersey, parking is not permitted within 25 feet of a crosswalk at an intersection.

Question 12 - Mock Exam

(A) At an intersection with a four-way stop, the vehicle that reached the intersection first is the one that proceeds first.

Question 13 - Mock Exam

(D) At an intersection without traffic controls, if two or more vehicles arrive around the same time, the vehicle on the right has the right of way.

Question 14 - Mock Exam

(A) Use available means and signals to communicate with other drivers. This includes hand signals, your vehicle's signals, or your vehicle's horn when necessary.

Question 15 - Mock Exam

(C) When a pedestrian is in a crosswalk, they always have the right-of-way, regardless of the light's color.

Question 16 - Mock Exam

(C) Both an entrance and an exit are possible on a weaving lane. Vehicles trying to access the expressway and those trying to leave it may collide as a result. Vehicles that are already on the expressway have the right-of-way in this case. Vehicles attempting to enter the highway must therefore give way to those attempting to exit.

Question 17 - Mock Exam

(C) In New Jersey, right turns on red are allowed, unless there are signs prohibiting it. However, you must first come to a complete stop and yield to both pedestrians and other traffic.

Question 18 - Mock Exam

(D) Before proceeding through an intersection, keep an eye out for approaching cars and people crossing to the left and right. When you are at a halt, take a quick glance to the left and the right before moving. Make sure your path through the intersection is clear by taking a second check across the intersection.

Question 19 - Mock Exam

(D) Large blind areas, or "No-Zones," are present in trucks and other large vehicles. A tractor-trailer's rear No-Zone can reach 200 feet beyond the truck. Keep a good distance behind a truck that is backing up or ready to start. Never follow too closely behind a truck or hang out between two trucks. Give a truck making a wide turn more room on the road. When you have to stop behind a vehicle, give yourself room, especially if you're going uphill. The truck may slide backward somewhat when it begins to move.

Question 20 - Mock Exam

(C) All drivers in New Jersey are required by law to stop for emergency vehicles when they sound their sirens or flash red, blue, or both red and blue emergency lights. When approaching an emergency vehicle, a driver should veer to the extreme right of the road, stop, and wait for it to pass. The driver must thereafter stay at least 300 feet behind an emergency vehicle flashing its lights. Unless instructed to do so by a fire, emergency rescue, or police authority, a driver should never park within 200 feet of an operational fire department truck or run over a fire hose.

Question 21 - Mock Exam

(B) In New Jersey, the usage of studded snow tires is allowed from November 15 through April 1. Nonetheless, the optimal traction on ice or deep, hard-packed snow is provided by tire chains.

Question 22 - Mock Exam

(B) If you start to slide, remain calm, slowly take your foot off the gas, and gently steer in the direction you want the car to go. Refrain from braking, particularly if your vehicle lacks an anti-lock braking system (ABS). This technique, called "steering into the skid". Once you regain control, straighten the wheels.

Question 23 - Mock Exam

(C) After navigating through water, gently pump your conventional disc and drum brakes to test and dry them. If you slam on the brakes, they could lock up.

Question 24 - Mock Exam

(C) If your windshield wipers suddenly stop during adverse weather, slow down, find a safe place off the road, and activate your hazard lights. Call for assistance if needed.

Question 25 - Mock Exam

(B) No-Zones are significant blind spots around large vehicles, including trucks, where smaller vehicles may vanish or get so close they inhibit the large vehicle's ability to safely stop or maneuver. The larger the vehicle, the bigger the No-Zones, which greatly increase the risk of accidents. While it's not always possible to avoid No-Zones, it's vital not to stay in them longer than necessary and never to follow a truck too closely.

Question 26 - Mock Exam

(C) On a curve, your vehicle tends to move in a straight line, which can lead to a skid, especially if you brake during the curve. To handle this, reduce your speed before entering the curve so you don't have to brake while in it.

Question 27 - Mock Exam

(B) According to New Jersey law, if you hold a basic driver license, you're allowed to use a hands-free cell phone, but not a handheld one. However, those in the Graduated Driver License (GDL) program are not permitted to use any cell phone, even a hands-free one.

Question 28 - Mock Exam

(B) To leave a highway, transition into the deceleration lane and start to reduce your speed, adhering to the advisory speed limit. This lane will guide you to an exit ramp.

Question 29 - Mock Exam

(D) If you're being tailgated, decrease your speed and signal the driver behind you to overtake. If this doesn't work, pull over, stop, and allow the tailgater to pass. Never try to speed up to pacify or distance yourself from a tailgater, as no speed will be too fast for some.

Question 30 - Mock Exam

(C) A left turn from a lane other than the far left is only permitted when signs, signals, or road markings allow it. Some major intersections have more than one lane designated for left turns.

Question 31 - Mock Exam

(A) It's imperative to adhere to the posted speed limit at all times. While it's recommended to keep pace with the flow of traffic, this should not be done if it requires exceeding the speed limit.

Question 32 - Mock Exam

(B) When a solid yellow line and a broken yellow line are present between opposing lanes, overtaking is prohibited if the solid yellow line is on your side.

Question 33 - Mock Exam

(C) A lane marked with white diamond symbols is a high-occupancy vehicle (HOV) lane. It's reserved for specific types of vehicles or those carrying multiple passengers. Watch for signs indicating which vehicles are permitted and at what times.

Question 34 - Mock Exam

(C) You should not shift gears when crossing railroad tracks as there's a risk your vehicle could stall. At railroad crossings, wait until there's space for your vehicle on the other side and yield to crossing trains.

Question 35 - Mock Exam

(A) A double solid yellow line denotes the center of the road, dividing traffic traveling in opposing directions. Passing is prohibited on both sides of the line, and the line may only be crossed to make a left turn.

Question 36 - Mock Exam

(A) Trucks and buses, due to their size, need more distance to slow down than cars. Maintaining a constant speed when overtaking and merging back in front of these larger vehicles is essential. Cutting in front of a truck or bus and suddenly reducing speed could result in a rear-end collision.

Question 37 - Mock Exam

(D) Heat can bring oil present in the asphalt to the surface, which can be loosened by rainwater, leading to slippery conditions. As more rain falls, the oil gets washed away, gradually restoring normal road traction.

Question 38 - Mock Exam

(D) As you turn your head to check your blind spots, it's important to keep the steering wheel straight. There's a natural inclination for people to move their arms in the direction their head turns.

Question 39 - Mock Exam

(B) On a two-way road without centerline markings, it's necessary to leave at least half the road for vehicles traveling in the opposite direction. Even when you cannot avoid driving left of the centerline, you must yield to oncoming traffic.

Question 40 - Mock Exam

(D) Drinking alcohol impairs a driver's senses and judgment. After consuming two to four drinks, reaction time, coordination, balance, vision, and distance judgment start to deteriorate, making driving unsafe. Only time can sober a person, as it allows the body to metabolize the alcohol, which is a slow process.

Question 41 - Mock Exam

(B) The solid white line marks the outer edge of the roadway and can only be crossed by vehicles entering or exiting the shoulder.

Question 42 - Mock Exam

(D) When driving at 50 mph on dry pavement, it will take approximately 247 feet to come to a complete stop.

Question 43 - Mock Exam

(D) A rectangular or diamond-shaped orange sign is used to identify a highway work zone.

Question 44 - Mock Exam

(B) When moving to New Jersey from another state with a car that is at least five years old, you must have it inspected within 14 days of registering it.

Question 45 - Mock Exam

(B) While waiting at a stop sign to turn right, if a vehicle approaching from the left has its turn signal on, you should wait until the other vehicle has actually started to turn before you begin your turn.

Question 46 - Mock Exam

(C) In New Jersey, it is generally not permitted to make a left turn at a red light.

Question 47 - Mock Exam

(D) During the New Jersey road test, you must provide all of the following documents: a valid permit, the vehicle's registration card, and the vehicle's insurance card.

Question 48 - Mock Exam

(D) Bicyclists, drivers of horse-drawn vehicles, riders on horses, inline skaters, skateboarders, moped drivers, and motorcyclists all have the same rights and obligations on the state's public roads as do automobile and truck drivers, according to New Jersey law.

Question 49 - Mock Exam

(B) If a tire blows out while driving, you should avoid braking immediately. Instead, grip the steering wheel firmly, steer straight ahead, and gradually release your foot off the gas pedal.

Question 50 - Mock Exam

(C) When you have already entered an intersection and the traffic light changes to yellow or red, you should follow through and clear the intersection, rather than stopping or making a turn.

A MESSAGE FROM THE DRIVING SCHOOL

As we wrap up this workbook, we just wanted to say a big thank you! We're so glad you chose us to be a part of your journey towards mastering the art of driving. It's been an absolute pleasure helping you get closer to acing that DMV exam.

We genuinely care about your success and satisfaction, and we're always looking for ways to make our resources better. That's where you come in - we'd love to hear your thoughts about this workbook.

Your feedback is like gold dust to us. It not only helps us improve, but it also guides future learners who are just starting out on their driving journey. So, if you have a spare moment, would you mind sharing your experience with this workbook?

Leaving a review is easy as pie. Just head over to where you bought the book and let us know what you think. Every single word you share matters to us, and we're really excited to hear about your learning journey.

Once again, a big thank you for picking our workbook. We're cheering you on and wishing you all the best as you hit the road and put all that learning into action. Safe driving and take care!

Thank you so much,

Drive Ready Publications

Made in the USA
Middletown, DE
06 September 2024

60365154R00102